MAD OR GOD?

What a wonderfully fresh and refreshing treatment of the life and personality of Jesus Christ, the greatest individual and centrepiece of human history. This book demonstrates both the wholeness of Jesus Christ – God become man – and the reality that he brings wholeness to those individuals who put their trust in him. Readers will find themselves irresistibly attracted to him in the pages of this book.
Lindsay Brown, Director, Lausanne Movement and former General Secretary, International Fellowship of Evangelical Students

Mad or God? is a unique and unusual book about Jesus, written by two Christian psychiatrists. Taking into account Jesus' mental state, consistency of life, character and relationships as portrayed in the gospels, Martinez and Sims show not only that there is a lack of evidence that Jesus was ever mentally unwell, but also that he should be considered to have had 'the healthiest mind of all'. If it was ever too easy to dismiss the claims of Jesus on the grounds that he must have been mad, this book makes it difficult again. Don't read it if you don't want to take Jesus seriously!
Professor Chris Cook, Durham University

A fresh and unconventional treatment of the 'mad, bad or God' trilemma, crafted by G. K. Chesterton (*The Everlasting Man*) and popularized by C. S. Lewis (*Mere Christianity*). This surprisingly touching book takes us on a fascinating journey into the psyche and character of Jesus of Nazareth. By looking at specific pathologies that they have observed and treated as clinicians, the authors expose the lofty but non-specific 'craziness' allegations of the New Atheists as lazy and unfounded assertions. But much more wonderfully, their investigation reveals the healthiest mind of the most attractive person ever to walk on Planet Earth – suggesting it would take more than a Jesus to invent this Jesus. It left this reader needing a quiet place to worship.
The Revd Richard M. Cunningham, Director, Universities and Colleges Christian Fellowship

If the question of the sanity of Jesus holds you back, then read this book. *Mad or God?* provides insight that only professional psychiatrists can bring. Prepare to be taken on a journey.
Sharon Dirckx, Oxford Centre for Christian Apologetics and author of Why? Looking at God, Evil and Personal Suffering

Fresh, arresting and helpful, *Mad or God?* is a highly original examination of the most challenging question posed to us as humans. Well worth reading and exploring.
Os Guinness, author of The Journey: A Thinking Person's Quest for Meaning

Finally, a credible, psychological investigation into the mind of Christ. Not only do Pablo and Andrew provide a compelling apologetic for the divine sonship of Jesus, but they also do much to educate the church compassionately about the nature of mental well-being. Through their understanding of Jesus' mind and emotions, the authors reveal a model of emotional discipleship that has long remained hidden from the Christian community. Their work will provide conviction, assurance and hope for many.
The Revd Will van der Hart, Director, The Mind and Soul Foundation

Mad or God? – a highly original examination of the mental landscape of Jesus – is written by authors with vast clinical experience. It provides believers with fresh insight into the Person of Jesus, and will be useful in drawing sceptics to consider Christ. Very highly recommended!
Becky Manley Pippert, author and presenter of Empowered: Equipping Everyone for Relational Evangelism

Two eminent psychiatrists, who have a lifetime's experience in the diagnosis and treatment of mental disorders, apply their skills to the question of Jesus' mental health with astounding conclusions. Drawing deeply on the Gospel accounts of Christ's life and ministry, they find not the slightest shadow of mental imbalance but, instead, a mind without parallel in history. The coherence of his discourse, the ethical richness of his teachings, the profound influence of his words and the depth of his relationships point to his true identity and explain his life-transforming power. A masterly blend of clinical wisdom, biblical exposition and personal testimony.
Peter Saunders, Chief Executive, Christian Medical Fellowship

PABLO MARTINEZ
& ANDREW SIMS

MAD OR GOD?

JESUS: THE HEALTHIEST MIND OF ALL

INTER-VARSITY PRESS
36 Causton Street, London SW1P 4ST, England
Email: ivp@ivpbooks.com
Website: www.ivpbooks.com

First published 2018

British Library Cataloguing-in-Publication Data
A catalogue record for this book is available from the British Library.

ISBN: 978–1–78359–605–8
eBook ISBN: 978–1–78359–606–5

Set in Dante 12/15 pt
Typeset in Great Britain by CRB Associates, Potterhanworth, Lincolnshire

Inter-Varsity Press publishes Christian books that are true to the Bible and that communicate the gospel, develop discipleship and strengthen the church for its mission in the world.

IVP originated within the Inter-Varsity Fellowship, now the Universities and Colleges Christian Fellowship, a student movement connecting Christian Unions in universities and colleges throughout Great Britain, and a member movement of the International Fellowship of Evangelical Students. Website: www.uccf.org.uk. That historic association is maintained, and all senior IVP staff and committee members subscribe to the UCCF Basis of Faith.

CONTENTS

FOREWORD

One of the most popular ways of dismissing the existence of God, particularly the supernatural God of the Bible, is to dismiss him as a delusion. This is the thesis of the best-seller *The God Delusion* by Richard Dawkins. Dawkins, who chooses Christianity as his main target, regards not only God as a delusion but the whole of Christianity as 'barking mad'. Such accusations are not new: Jesus himself was accused of demon possession, the Christian apostle Paul of madness, and more recently Sigmund Freud held that 'religion is comparable to a childhood neurosis'.[1]

When I first read Dawkins' book, the first thought that struck me was that his bold title was making a claim that really belonged to the realm of psychiatry, yet Dawkins was not a psychiatrist. The topic was outside his expertise. Indeed, it was also outside mine, and so I thought the only reasonable thing to do was to see what had been said and written by professional psychiatrists. In the course of my research I came across the work of Professor Andrew Sims, a former President of the Royal College of Psychiatrists and one of the authors of the present volume. Reading Sims' excellent book *Is Faith Delusion?* I discovered that, for someone who claims to put great store by scientific evidence, Dawkins displays culpable ignorance of the considerable body of research showing the positive contribution of Christianity to well-being.

After many years' research, Sims concluded,

> The advantageous effect of religious belief and spirituality on mental and physical health is one of the best-kept secrets in psychiatry and medicine generally. If the findings of the huge volume of research on this topic had gone in the opposite direction and it had been found that religion damages your mental health, it would have been front-page news in every newspaper in the land.[2]

Sims cites as evidence the *American Journal of Public Health* major meta-analysis of epidemiological studies on the psychological effects of religious belief:

> In the majority of studies, religious involvement is correlated with well-being, happiness and life satisfaction; hope and optimism; purpose and meaning in life; higher self-esteem; better adaptation to bereavement; greater social support and less loneliness; lower rates of depression and faster recovery from depression; lower rates of suicide and fewer positive attitudes towards suicide; less anxiety; less psychosis and fewer psychotic tendencies; lower rates of alcohol and drug use and abuse; less delinquency and criminal activity; greater marital stability and satisfaction . . . We concluded that for the vast majority of people the apparent benefit of devout religious belief and practice probably outweigh the risks.[3]

We read the New Atheists in vain to find even a hint of awareness of this 'huge volume of research'. Their vaunted commitment to science is not quite all that it seems.

In the present volume Sims joins forces with fellow psychiatrist Pablo Martinez to address a central question that, in my view, has, up until now, not received anything like the treatment it deserves. It is not the Freud-inspired question of whether or not God is a delusion, but the specifically Christian, yet related, question of the mental health and stability of Christ himself. After all, the central claim of Christianity is that God became human, 'the Word became flesh' (John 1:14), in the person of Jesus Christ. Consistent with that, Jesus said, 'I and the Father are one' (John 10:30). The obvious question to ask is: what does the making of such a claim imply for the psychological status of the one who makes it?

The initial stimulus to the authors' investigation is C. S. Lewis's famous statement about such 'off-the-scale' claims of this kind:

> A man who was merely a man and said the sort of things Jesus said would not be a great moral teacher. He would either be a lunatic – on a level with the man who says he is a poached egg – or else he would be the devil of hell. You can shut him up for a fool, you can spit at him and kill him as a demon; or you can fall at his feet and call him Lord and God.[4]

The authors' objective is to use their expertise in psychiatry to investigate the first of these options.

The importance of this issue can scarcely be exaggerated for the very obvious reason that it has to do with the truth or falsity of the Christian faith. For, if there were any grounds for suspecting that Jesus was mentally unbalanced or unstable, then, of course, the whole Christian edifice comes crashing to the ground.

Martinez and Sims have spent their whole lives dealing with men and women who have exhibited the whole range of human mental behaviour, and they have treated the most strange and intransigent mental conditions. Their assessment of such people involves at least five important aspects: character, life (the coherence of words and deeds), relationships, reaction to adversity and influence on people, criteria that they now use to look at the person of Jesus. At each point the authors ensure that we understand precisely what they mean by the particular aspect of mental life in question by giving us examples from their extensive clinical experience.

Their considered conclusion is that 'no mentally sick person, or no evil man, would ever have been able to speak or behave in the impeccable and influential way that Jesus did, unless he really was what he claimed to be: God'.

The book takes us on a journey, not into a geographical landscape but into a mental landscape, and involves us not merely in getting to know a set of new facts but in getting to know a person. We are all aware that on the purely human level, getting to know another person cannot be done from a distance, objectively without involvement. You will never get to know me if you rest content with scientific investigations involving medical probes, computed tomography (CT), PET scans and the like. You will have to give up your distance and engage me in conversation, in the hope that I reveal something of myself to you. Our understanding of each other will deepen only as mutual trust develops.

It is so with Jesus. It is only as we find ourselves coming closer to him that we begin to see the sheer wonder and balance of his personality, the lucidity, peace and tranquillity of his mind in the most adverse of circumstances. It becomes increasingly clear why and how he has become a source of mental peace and stability, freedom from neurosis and positive health and salvation for millions of people throughout history. The discovery of what they call the 'healthiest mind of all' has inspired trust in Christ in the authors.

As I journeyed along with them, I found that their unusual perspective illuminated many aspects of the Lord's person in a way that I had not seen before. It also increased my awareness of the many different kinds and the complexity of various mental issues with which people are faced.

This book represents an important contribution to the evidence that Jesus is, as he claimed to be, the incarnate Son of God. I am sure it will help to open many readers' eyes to the wonder of the person of Christ, and refresh and renew their faith and strengthen their confidence in him.

Professor John Lennox
Professor of Mathematics (emeritus)
at the University of Oxford
and Fellow in Mathematics and the Philosophy of Science
at Green Templeton College, Oxford

PREFACE

*I cannot believe that a madman [Jesus] could have
touched and inspired the lives of millions of people.*

This was the reply of Bono, lead singer of U2, when he was
interviewed by Gay Byrne on Irish television about his faith
in Jesus. His words echo the experience of many others who
have seen their lives changed by the person and the message
of the Master of Galilee.

Why did Jesus exert – and does he continue to exert – such
a power of fascination over men and women, a fascination
that captivates Christians and non-Christians alike? Could a
mentally sick man ever have such an astonishing influence on
people's lives?

What magnetic attraction, what amazing power, lies
behind Jesus, causing a man like Dostoevsky to say, 'If
someone proved to me that Christ is outside the truth and
that in reality the truth were outside of Christ, then I should
prefer to remain with Christ rather than with the truth'?[1]

Was the Jesus of the Gospels mad, or was he really, as he
and his followers claimed, the Son of God? C. S. Lewis pointed
to the core of the problem when he wrote the extract quoted
on p. xi by Professor John Lennox in the Foreword to this

book. This famous quotation, known as the 'trilemma', inspired and motivated us to write these pages.[2]

The purpose of this book is to examine mainly one of the first two options that Lewis raised. Was Jesus mentally deranged? Is there evidence to conclude that he was a megalomaniac whose words have therefore no more value than the message of an insane person? As psychiatrists, we want to respond to these questions because the insanity of Jesus is one of the arguments that the New Atheists use today to mock Christianity. We cannot remain silent when our professional experience enables and equips us to offer a robust defence of Jesus' mental health.

We will be doing some detective work throughout the book in order to solve a mystery. Where is the key to understanding the puzzling combination of 'egocentricity' and humility, servanthood and the astounding claims of Jesus? This is an intriguing paradox that requires enquiry: the striking discrepancy between the self-giving of his life and the self-centredness of his teaching, the humility of the servant and the greatness of the Lord. Jesus believed he was unique, but this self-consciousness is not at all explained in terms of narcissism or megalomania. There must be deeper reasons that go beyond any psychological analysis.

We, the authors, made this enquiry years ago. These pages are basically a reflection of the personal journey that led us to discover that this great paradox contains, like hidden treasure, the clue to understanding the uniqueness of Jesus' life and work. Such a discovery went beyond an intellectual response and became a personal encounter that, for both of us in different countries and at different times, transformed our lives completely.

The writers of the Gospels tell us that, when a person confronts the life of Jesus, they see something glorious: the glory of God's character as far as it can be expressed in a man. After three years with his Master, John, the disciple closest to Jesus, summarizes his experience with forceful words: 'We have beheld his glory, glory as of the only Son from the Father' (John 1:14, RSV). This is the same glorious character that we, like millions of people, discovered, because the powerful fascination of Jesus continues to shine and attract today every bit as much as it did 2,000 years ago.

The Roman centurion who commanded the execution of Jesus exclaimed in amazement right after his death, 'Surely he was the Son of God!' (Matthew 27:54).

May you, our readers, come to a similar experience, and not only be convinced that Jesus had the healthiest mind of all, but also be attracted by his glorious character.

Pablo Martinez and Andrew Sims

ACKNOWLEDGMENTS

Most of the important things we know about mental illness and its treatment, and what it feels like to the sufferer, we have learnt from our patients. We thank them for this and we respect them for the hardship they have endured.

There are many individuals whom we wish to thank for inspiration and focus in writing this book. We wish to thank our editor, Eleanor Trotter, for her insistence on our holding the readers in the forefront of our minds during the writing process, and for her encouragement throughout; we thank Professor John Lennox for his support and for encouraging our belief that the subject of this book matters; we thank our readers, Dr David Sims, Samuel Bunn and Rosie Bunn, who have each contributed to the eventual shape and tone of *Mad or God?* We would also like to thank Marta Martinez and Ruth Sims, who have helped us in more ways than they realize.

INTRODUCTION

Exploring a life story is exciting: like starting a journey to an unknown land. This book is a journey through the life of Jesus from a psychiatric perspective. We invite you to join us for a trip with nine stops. Each stop becomes a test to evaluate specific facets of his character.

In the first part (chapters 1–3), the journey takes us through terrain that may sound quite new to you. Our aim is to offer evidence that Jesus' mind suffered from no mental illness. By the end of the third stop you will see that Jesus was not just normal in terms of mental health, but significantly above normal.

Then, following the logic of C. S. Lewis's 'trilemma', we will embark on the second part of our journey. We now move from the negative to the positive: if Jesus was *not* mentally deranged, then we need to prove that he was indeed a man endowed with an extraordinary mental stability and an unquestionable moral uprightness. So the purpose of the second part (chapters 4–9) is to provide evidence that Jesus appears before us with the 'healthiest mind of all' and the most balanced and righteous life.

On this journey we will not be covering properly the second option of the Lewis trilemma: 'he would be the devil of hell'. The issue of Jesus' moral goodness would require a whole book in itself. Nevertheless, human beings are a unity, and the moral and the emotional cannot be separated into isolated compartments. This is why we will often refer to this option too, because Jesus' uprightness asserts itself vigorously in a natural way as we consider his life and his work.

The stops in the second part of our trip will allow us to contemplate the person of Jesus through five different windows: his character, his life (the coherence of his words and deeds), his relationships, his reaction to adversity and his influence on people. These various perspectives provide us with an accurate assessment of a person's stability. By the end of the journey we will reach the conclusion that no mentally sick person, or no evil man, would ever have been able to speak or behave in the impeccable and influential way that Jesus did, unless he really was what he claimed to be: God.

What luggage do you need for this trip? The conclusion above requires not only intellectual acceptance, but personal commitment. This is why your luggage can be summarized in one simple word: trust. Trust is the personal background from which we see the Jesus of our study.

But why is trust a key prerequisite? We believe that Jesus is not merely an object of scientific research that you can dissect in the laboratory of so-called scholarly studies, but a person with whom you can establish a relationship. The starting point for any relationship is a minimum level of trust. In the study of Jesus, intellectual persuasion, rational analysis based on arguments, is important, but it is not enough. For this reason we have deliberately chosen the world of faith. We believe – and have experienced – that faith (trust) opens the eyes of our understanding. The more you believe, the more you are enabled to see. So in the background of our approach, 'seeing is believing' becomes 'believing leads to seeing'.

Trust has also determined the sources that we have used: the Gospels.[1] They are the natural source for any study on the character of Jesus. We believe that 'the Gospels can and should be accepted . . . at least as an honest attempt to say what happened'.[2]

From the first chapter you will discover that Jesus has always been an object of controversy. Why does he not leave anyone indifferent? Why does he provoke such opposite reactions? The reason lies in the question he asked his disciples: 'Who do you say I am?' It is not a naive question springing from mere curiosity. Jesus wants people to define themselves in the light of his claims and character. 'The fact of Christ is not just a fact of history; it has become also a fact of conscience . . . We had thought intellectually to examine him; we find he is spiritually examining us.'[3]

If Jesus' claims are true, then it is not enough to be 'amazed at him', as many of his contemporaries were, because he wants not to be admired, but to be followed.

We are aware that this journey is not free from dangers. For this reason an important word of clarification is necessary here. Although the nature and purpose of the book will lead us to focus mainly on Jesus as a man, we do not see him as *only* a man. Thus, we want to acknowledge from the beginning that we believe Jesus was *fully God* and *fully human* at the same time. The two-natures Christology is the context from which we write with an unhesitant commitment to this fundamental truth of historic Christianity: he was, and is, truly God and man in one person.[4]

The danger lies in the fact that we are faced here with a supernatural and perfect synthesis, and it is not always easy to keep a perfect balance when describing these two sides of the truth. For this reason, our working assumption is not to examine Jesus as a man only, but also to dig into his claims as Saviour and Lord. Throughout the book we follow the so-called 'Christology from below', the inductive method which takes as its starting point that which was said and done by Jesus himself. This journey leads us progressively upwards to the highest peak (in chapter 9), where the witness of Jesus about his own person illuminates how this true man was also truly God.

Along the journey the perfect humanity of Jesus becomes the prelude that leads us to grasp the full symphony of his divinity. In our own lives, Jesus the man became one day Christ, our Lord, enabling us to affirm personally the 'two-natures Christology', namely, that Jesus is much more than a man; he is 'the image of the invisible God' (Colossians 1:15).

If you want a glimpse of what lies ahead, it will take only a few seconds: go to the contents and read the subtitles of each chapter carefully. They are intended to summarize the substance of the book in a few memorable sentences, like milestones on the trip. Except for chapter 1, they are all literal quotations from the Bible, referring to Jesus or pronounced by Jesus himself. We hope these signposts on the journey will help you remember, and reflect on, the most essential aspects of the person of Jesus.

May your journey be filled with challenging experiences. Enjoy it, but above all enjoy the protagonist, Jesus, who said, 'I have come that they may have life, and have it to the full' (John 10:10).

1. THE TEST OF PSYCHIATRY: WAS JESUS MENTALLY DISTURBED?

This man we are talking about either was (and is) just what he said, or else a lunatic, or something worse.
C. S. Lewis

Jesus has had a greater influence than any other person on individuals, and on history. Indeed, 2,000 years after his death the number of his followers continues to increase. During his lifetime he met with violent hatred and a shameful death. Now his followers are still persecuted and martyred in many parts of the world, and they encounter verbal attack and discrimination in many others. For those who know Jesus, he is everything; for those who do not, all possible means have been used to discredit him.

'He's raving mad. Why listen to him?' his critics have been protesting for 2,000 years, and still insist today. Some say that Jesus is mad because they do not understand him, some because they reject him, and some have just never tried or bothered to listen.

What did he really say about himself? Could it be construed as the outpouring of a madman?

Why does it matter whether or not Jesus was mentally ill?

A powerful businessman became increasingly bombastic, noisy and rude to employees, clients and shareholders. He made decisions with long-lasting consequences arbitrarily and without consulting his colleagues. Others in the firm realized that he was mentally ill and tried in all possible ways to keep him from public view. They realized that his authority and power would immediately be undermined if there was even a whiff of mental illness.

Why does it matter whether Jesus was mad or not? It matters because Jesus offers meaning, trust and credibility, authority, and a relationship built on love. If the view that Jesus is mad can be substantiated, then all of these disappear. To convince us that Jesus was psychiatrically deranged, there would have to be signs suggesting one or other of three groups of mental illnesses: psychosis (considered in chapter 2), other mental illness or personality disorder (considered in chapter 3).

When Jesus said of himself, 'I am the good shepherd' (John 10:11), that phrase, like so much else that he said, carried many associated meanings for his Jewish hearers because of their knowledge of the Old Testament: the coming king who will free us from Roman oppression, the promised Messiah, national and personal security, and self-respect. Some accepted him, but others said, 'He is demon-possessed and raving mad. Why listen to him?' (John 10:20). When Jesus spoke, this immediately attracted his critics, often with some religious authority, to launch into accusations of madness in order to undermine his credentials.

Really the Messiah?

The claim by his detractors that he was mad was inextricably linked to the realization that Jesus was the Messiah. The first hint was made by the Magi (wise men) at the time of his birth when they came to worship 'the one who has been born king of the Jews' (Matthew 2:2). This was an extraordinary endorsement from heathen scholars when greeting a baby!

The expression 'Son of God', which implies 'Messiah', is first used in Matthew's Gospel by two demon-possessed men who shouted at Jesus (Matthew 8:29). They recognized that Jesus' healing power came from God and that he was able to heal them from madness and violence.

When Jesus enabled Peter to walk on the water and calmed the storm on the lake, the disciples said to him, with grateful conviction, 'Truly you are the Son of God' (Matthew 14:33). Jesus put these questions to his disciples: ' "Who do people say the Son of Man is? . . . But what about you? . . . Who do you say I am?" Simon Peter answered: "You are the Messiah, the Son of the living God" ' (Matthew 16:13–16).

At Jesus' trial the high priest said to him, 'I charge you under oath by the living God: Tell us if you are the Messiah, the Son of God' (Matthew 26:63). In his reply Jesus accepted the claim. Finally, a centurion at the foot of the cross, in terror from the earthquake, said, 'Surely he was the Son of God!' (Matthew 27:54).

These witnesses came from different backgrounds and had differing opinions about Jesus, but all queried whether Jesus was indeed the Son of God, and therefore the Messiah. In Mark's Gospel, hints that Jesus was the Messiah were linked with his imminent death.[1] Jesus, and his disciples, claiming that he was the Messiah was not a boast, but proved to be a death warrant. For the Jewish leaders, declaring him mad was their only effective means to stop the spreading idea that he was the Messiah.

From early on in his ministry his disciples had come to realize that Jesus was 'the Messiah'. Jesus himself believed this. He applied the Old Testament Scriptures about the 'Suffering Servant' and 'God coming into his kingdom' to himself, and, in so doing, he 'was to court the charge of madness'.[2] Jesus fulfilled the Old Testament prophecies about the Messiah: a descendant of Eve, from the seed of Abraham, a prophet like Moses, a king like David, a priest like Melchizedek, the servant of the Lord and the Son of man.[3]

'Jesus is crazy' is of course a cheap form of abuse, a deliberate put-down by those who want to dismiss him. Yet what he said and did was like no-one else throughout history. How do we explain his behaviour on earth, acting as a great leader, and his reputation since his death, the most venerated person of all time? Some of the statements that led to the accusation of madness were: 'your sins are forgiven', 'the kingdom of God is coming', 'the King of the Jews' and 'today this Scripture is fulfilled in your hearing'. And he supported these colossal claims with the whole manner of his life.

C. S. Lewis's 'trilemma' implies that either (1) what Jesus said is true, or (2) he is a liar, a fraud, or (3) a madman. As we said in the introduction, in this book we deal mainly with the claim that he was mad. Jesus shouted,

> Whoever believes in me does not believe in me only, but
> in the one who sent me. The one who looks at me is seeing
> the one who sent me. I have come into the world as a light,
> so that no one who believes in me should stay in darkness . . .
> I did not speak on my own, but the Father who sent me
> commanded me to say all that I have spoken. I know that

his command leads to eternal life. So whatever I say is just
what the Father has told me to say.
(John 12:44–46, 49–50)

Jesus was not just a philosopher producing wise sayings for
discussion among the intelligentsia. He claims to be speaking
directly from God. As theologian and writer N. T. (Tom)
Wright says, 'The real reason for doubt is the shuddering fear
that it is after all true. What if Jesus really were the mouthpiece
of the living God? What if seeing him really did mean seeing
the father?'[4] What a terrifying idea! It is more comfortable to
assume he is mad. In his lifetime some of his closest friends
betrayed and denied him, and most people couldn't really
make him out. He was compelling but puzzling.[5] But was
he mad?

What is mental illness?

We now apply the principles of psychiatry to Jesus' story.
What is mental illness, mental disorder? For such questions
to have any meaning, there has to be a clear threshold between
normal experience and 'caseness' – mental disorder. Speech
and behaviour that appears to be unintelligible does not
necessarily indicate mental illness. If I cannot understand
someone, that does not prove that person to be insane – it
could even be something lacking in me!

Anna was a grandmother, with her stable and supportive
family around her. She was active in her community and
church. Her habits were regular, including completing the
newspaper crossword every morning at breakfast. Inexplicably,
she began to slow down and become very quiet. She became
gloomy, grumpy, quite unlike her usual bright self, and gave
up many of her activities. She had no appetite and had lost a

lot of weight. She became apathetic and indecisive; she would sit still in her chair all day. Her family was very worried about her, and her doctor diagnosed depression and, because of her extreme weight loss, arranged for her to be admitted to hospital. There the diagnosis was confirmed, and appropriate treatment started. She began to improve and after a few months returned to her old self – picking up her previous activities and once more finishing the crossword every morning. She had suffered from a serious, potentially lethal, mental illness. Yet, following diagnosis and treatment, she made a full recovery.

June was the vicar of a small country parish. Towards the end of a long winter, she described everything as 'going pear-shaped'. The churchwarden had a blazing row with another member of the congregation and promptly resigned. The treasurer had a serious illness and was absent from church for several months. The head teacher of the village school, of which June was a governor, had to take leave in the middle of the term. June's husband had been working away from home for a few weeks, and her teenage son had given up on school work and was out most evenings. By April, June was completely exhausted, anxious and dejected; she felt that she could not take much more. After Easter she and her family had ten days' holiday with her sister who lived in Spain, and away from home she felt much better. Despite her gloom and tension in March, June never suffered from a mental illness. Throughout, her body and mind were reacting appropriately to the almost intolerable demands being made upon her at that stressful time, and when the outside pressures were removed, there came a blessed relief from symptoms. If you had talked to June in late March, you would probably have thought that she was mentally ill, but this was not so.

We will focus strongly on diagnosis over the next few chapters. There is no single 'mental illness'; there are many different psychiatric conditions, with varying features. How did the patient's condition arise? What other states of mind are similar, and, most importantly of all, what is likely to happen in the future and, therefore, what should be done about it?

Diagnosis is a means of communication between doctors and others, and it is based on the 'symptoms' and 'signs' that the sufferer shows.[6] The patient complains of symptoms, but physical signs are discovered on examination. In psychiatry, the complaints of the patient (feeling anxious) and observation by the clinician (agitation and tremor) are both described as symptoms, and added together to form signs of the diagnosis, anxiety disorder. The importance of diagnosis in psychiatry has increased as effective treatments have been developed.

Each mental illness shows a definite pattern, and illness is neither random nor arbitrary; what is said and done has meaning which may not be immediately apparent to the sufferer or the doctor. For example, depressive illness has a pattern, distinctive features, which are different from those of anorexia nervosa, because the symptoms that the sufferer describes, the onset of the condition, its course over time and its outcome, all differ. In the same way, the condition called schizophrenia differs radically from Alzheimer's disease, the most frequent type of dementia. There are clear, established patterns for the different conditions, and a variation from these is exceptional rather than usual. To claim that someone is mentally ill, one must describe which symptoms and signs of which specific mental disorder a patient is demonstrating.

Features of mental illness

There are four features common to all mental illnesses:

1. symptoms (what distresses the sufferer, as noted above)
2. loss of function (inability to carry out normal activities)
3. disturbance of relationships (family, friends, work)
4. disturbance in self-image (how patients feel about themselves).

Symptoms include both the complaints that the sufferer makes, and signs – indicators of mental disorder apparent on examination but not complained of by the patient. For example, slowness of speech and limited gesture in severe depression are signs, often more noticeable to the doctor than the patient.

A psychiatrist seeks to understand the patient's mental illness by observing carefully and taking a full and relevant history. Symptoms are explored with an emphasis on what it means for the sufferer. There is much more to the distress of depression than the phrase: 'I feel rather down.' How long has it been going on? How severe is it? Does anything particular bring it on? Does it cause physical symptoms? Many other relevant questions come into play. The aim of the psychiatrist is to understand the person – almost from within: what does it feel like inside you?

On asking about the loss of ability to function normally and harmoniously, one would enquire about the patient's situation – at home, at work, in his or her accustomed social group, for example, at church. There is almost always some problem in day-to-day functioning in all mental illnesses, but in a different manner for each condition. The person with severe depression feels unable to love or be loved at home, cannot carry out work effectively and finds going to outside events, such as church, intolerable. He or she often has very low self-esteem, and this adds to the other disabilities.

Relationships are disturbed in different ways, but in all mental illnesses this causes distress not only to the sufferers, but to all those around them. Some degree of alteration in how they feel about themselves almost always occurs with any mental illness.

Mental illnesses differ in all significant respects: cause, onset, course, treatment, outcome, degree of stigma it attracts and so on. However, being unusual or eccentric does not, in and of itself, constitute mental illness: recognizable features of a defined psychiatric condition must be present. The authors both know several eccentric people who are not mentally ill, because they experience no distress, nor do they cause others distress, and they function well with the demands society makes on them. Even the authors themselves may be somewhat odd! Just to be unusual, or even greatly disapproved of, does not make you mentally ill.

More than one psychiatric condition may be present at the same time. This is called co-morbidity, and it is frequently found among the mentally ill. Michael had a serious drink problem and was sacked by his employer. Consequently, he tried to drown himself in the sea. After his rescue and admission to hospital, he was found to be suffering from alcohol misuse *and* depressive illness.

Although it is most obvious with psychotic illness, some impairment of judgment occurs with any mental illness. It is this impairment of judgment that has been used to 'explain away' Jesus' teaching: in the mind of disparagers, mental illness = loss of judgment = ignore, and do not trust. We have to grasp Jesus' meaning from his words and his actions. He was truly man, 'fully human in every way' (Hebrews 2:17) –

he experienced the full range of human emotions. There is a lot of material, and surely enough has been written for two psychiatrists to know whether or not he suffered from any mental illness!

Meaning

We are all looking for meaning, but, significantly, without God's help, we cannot see meaning in Jesus, and therefore he must be 'mad', a 'crackpot' or a fanatic. To those who do not know him, his teaching appears to be the craziest thing – 'love your enemies' (Luke 6:27). He teaches exuberant and even self-destructive generosity – 'Give to everyone who asks you, and if anyone takes what belongs to you, do not demand it back' (Luke 6:30). He is even generous to the stingy and the wicked (Luke 6:35). This turns the world upside down. Not surprisingly, some think that the teaching, and therefore the person, is mad. But does his teaching make any sense? In his life and in all he said, Jesus was focused, directed and unambiguous. There was one clear goal: building his kingdom. Jesus' life and teaching might seem crazy, but how do we decide if it really is madness or mental illness? We will consider this in detail in the next chapter. Psychiatrists make their assessment on whether mental illness is present by making a careful enquiry into speech, behaviour and experience: 'If I were inside your mind, what would it be like?' This exploration of meaning for the individual is called 'descriptive phenomenology', and it is an acquired skill that all psychiatrists need in order to be effective.

There was purpose and meaning both in Jesus coming into the world: 'that by believing you may have life in his name' (John 20:31), and in his leaving the world. Jesus' vocation, what he states as his reason for coming, was to fulfil the Old

Testament prophecies for the 'Messiah', the Saviour: atonement and sacrifice for the whole world by crucifixion (the method of death for a violent criminal) of an innocent man. A battle was won, not by physical force, but by the power of love: 'Having loved his own who were in the world, he loved them to the end' (John 13:1). As we will consider in more detail later (in chapter 7), Jesus' sense of purpose and obedience to his Father is the only valid explanation for the whole sequence of events, starting in the garden of Gethsemane with his arrest, until his death on the cross, his burial and resurrection.

The meaning of Jesus' life was to do his Father's will: 'I did not speak on my own, but the Father who sent me commanded me to say all that I have spoken. I know that his command leads to eternal life' (John 12:49–50).

So was Jesus mentally ill? The best way to answer that is to find out what meaning Jesus invested in the events of his life, his words and his actions.

Misunderstanding

Why did people then, as they do now, declare that Jesus was mad? Because they misunderstood, and still misunderstand, what he was saying. They did not grasp his meaning and turned the spiritual into the physical. Still today we find this distinction difficult. They failed to see how what he said gave meaning to life, eternal life. And our generation still fails to see that.

So those who heard Jesus often misunderstood him. For example, much of what he said to the Samaritan woman at the well about 'living water' she misunderstood (John 4:10). Tom Wright puts it like this: 'Again and again . . . Jesus talks to people [and they] misunderstand what he says. He is talking at the heavenly level, and they are listening at the earthly level.'[7] Jesus upset comfortable conventions – his hearers did not like that, and said that he was mad.

These 'misunderstandings' often appear to be deliberate on Jesus' part. He knew what the other person was thinking, but he wanted to challenge his hearers with the life-changing consequences of his arrival into the world and the coming of the kingdom of God. In his exchange with Martha, Jesus said,

> 'Your brother will rise again.'
> Martha answered, 'I know he will rise again in the resurrection at the last day.'
> Jesus said to her, 'I am the resurrection and the life. The one who believes in me will live, even though they die.'
> (John 11:23–25)

Incidentally, here Jesus is clearly pointing to his divine character, one of the two natures mentioned earlier, fully God and fully human at the same time.

Misunderstandings occur because Jesus is working at a different level. He remains focused on the kingdom of heaven. He teaches many things that contrast 'spirit' with 'flesh' – the spiritual and the physical realms. Quite often Jesus is talking about spiritual values, and his hearers misunderstand the meaning as physical. For example,

> Jesus stood and said in a loud voice, 'Let anyone who is thirsty come to me and drink. Whoever believes in me, as Scripture has said, rivers of living water will flow from within them.'
> By this he meant the Spirit, whom those who believed in him were later to receive.
> (John 7:37–39)

But Jesus never says that spirit is good or eternal and flesh bad or ephemeral, nor that spirit is metaphorical and flesh literal: both are made by God and are part of our whole and undivided nature.

In everyday conversation we are used to talking about 'spirit': 'the team played with spirit'; 'there was a bad spirit in the office.' We recognize its importance. Jesus' teaching was not only spiritual, but also practical. For example, he was explicit concerning money: 'You cannot serve both God and Money' (Luke 16:13); 'If you have not been trustworthy in handling worldly wealth, who will trust you with true riches?' (Luke 16:11). This caused controversy in his time, and it still does. Both then and now, it is much more comfortable to say that it is crazy and ignore it. His message about money and other belongings is generosity itself: 'Freely you have received; freely give' (Matthew 10:8). Because Jesus was so different from us, it is hardly surprising that we have often missed his meaning, misunderstood him and found his teaching 'mad'.

But what does it matter if Jesus was mad or suffering from a mental illness? If he had been an innovative philosopher or had made life-changing discoveries in physics, his mental state would have been largely irrelevant. But neither was the case. He portrayed a new way of life, a new kingdom in this world, a new relationship with God and with other people, and a world order based on love. For these reasons, we need to know whether we are safe to trust him, and what the source of his authority was. Was it based on the shaky foundation of mental illness?

Trust

Many had, and still have, a longing to be able to trust Jesus: 'the common people heard him gladly' (Mark 12:37, KJV). In the Gospel of John there are three references to Nicodemus, a Pharisee and a ruler of the Jews, an intelligent, rational and prominent leader. In the first (John 3:2), Nicodemus is a seeker. He has heard about Jesus and he comes to him secretly. He opens the conversation by saying, 'We know that you are a teacher who has come from God. For no one could perform the signs you are doing if God were not with him.'

On the second occasion, he is supportive, but still sitting on the fence (John 7:51). At a meeting of the Pharisees, the Jewish leaders, he spoke up on Jesus' behalf and said, 'Does our law condemn a man without first hearing him to find out what he has been doing?' This was enough for him to be branded as a follower of Jesus by the other Pharisees. In the third reference, Nicodemus was identified as a 'disciple' and he helped prepare Jesus' dead body for burial (John 19:39). From seeker to follower, what a remarkable transformation! Nicodemus, who had realized that Jesus had come from God, discovers rational and informed faith. He finds Jesus trustworthy and commits his life to him.

If Jesus had been mentally ill or emotionally unstable, he would not have commanded this confidence, whereby disciples, such as Nicodemus, Peter and many others, trusted him, literally, with their lives (see chapter 6). Jesus did not waver; he was focused on his ultimate destiny. Throughout the Gospel accounts there are at first hints, and then increasingly definite forecasts of his approaching death and the future establishment of the kingdom. Never was anyone so consistently goal-directed! There are clear signs and predictions of his death and resurrection, and his triumph over death, throughout his ministry.

Many people believed Jesus because of what he said and did. When he turned water into wine in Cana of Galilee, 'his disciples believed in him' (John 2:11). At the healing of the nobleman's son, 'Jesus had said to him [the father], "Your son will live." So he and his whole household believed' (John 4:53–54).

After the feeding of the 5,000, the crowd intended to make him king by force, but he withdrew to a mountain by himself (John 6:14–15). He would not be deflected from his ultimate goal to do his Father's will. Mounting conflict becomes increasingly clear in the story of the healing on the Sabbath of the man born blind (John 9:32–33). In exasperation, the man himself eventually says to the Pharisees, 'Nobody has ever heard of opening the eyes of a man born blind. If this man were not from God, he could do nothing.' At the time of the raising of Lazarus, Jesus says to Martha, 'Did I not tell you that if you believe, you will see the glory of God?' (John 11:40). Then, just before it takes place, Jesus tells his disciples about his forthcoming death and resurrection, suffering and new birth. This sequence of events was all quite conscious and deliberate on Jesus' part.

Was he mad or suicidal to act step by step in such a way that it ultimately and inevitably resulted in his death by crucifixion, or was he the Son of God carrying out the will of his Father?

Mental illness undermines trustworthiness. Jack was admitted to hospital after being found unconscious in his garage with the car engine running and a pipe leading to it from the exhaust. A neighbour, knowing that Jack was on his own, had just 'happened to look in' and heard the engine. Jack's was a very sad story. He had suffered severe mood swings for many years, but had not previously sought help. When he was 'high', he was quarrelsome and extravagant with his money, repeatedly getting into debt. When he was 'down', he was morose, bad-tempered, apathetic and unreliable in his commitments. Dawn, his wife, had adored him from their first meeting at a mutual friend's wedding. She still loved him, but she could no longer stand his fighting and profligate spending when high, or his prolonged, unrelieved misery when low. She confided, 'I still love him, but I can no longer live with him because I cannot trust him from one day to the next.' Jack could not live without her, and that explained his attempted suicide. Sadly, mental illness undermines trust.

Jesus, by contrast, was utterly trustworthy. At his trial, before his crucifixion, he said, 'The reason I was born and came into the world is to testify to the truth. Everyone on the side of truth listens to me' (John 18:37). The course of his earthly life was based on God's authority and quite deliberately directed towards his ultimate goal.

Authority

Authority was vital for the chief priests and Jewish leaders during Jesus' ministry, and it is just as vital today: '"Tell us by what authority you are doing these things," they said. "Who gave you this authority?"' (Luke 20:2). John the Baptist had declared Jesus to be the Messiah, but the leaders were ambiguous about John. Was he from God? Was he a true prophet? Jesus 'taught as one who had authority, and not as their teachers of the law' (Matthew 7:29). He showed it in all he did, and everyone who had dealings with him was aware of it.

His authority came from God and reflected his close relationship with his 'Father'. He had authority over both demons and sickness (Luke 4:31–42). Jesus commanded and rebuked demons (verse 35), rebuked the fever (verse 39) and forbade demons to speak (verse 41). His authority over demons emanated from their knowing that he was indeed the Messiah.

So he taught with authority, but often also with whimsical humour, which made his teaching more accessible – a friend might not get out of bed to give a loaf of bread for friendship's sake, but might respond to irritating nagging (Luke 11:5–8). When talking about God giving us the Holy Spirit, he uses the illustration of a good father giving gifts: if his son asks for a fish, he will not give a snake (Luke 11:11), or for an egg, a scorpion (verse 12). This authority, with a gentle touch, is further evidence of a healthy mind, and quite unlike the autocratic, 'paranoid' authority of a dictator.

The ultimate example of Jesus' authority was the command to his followers – his disciples then, his church now: 'Love each other as I have loved you' (John 15:12). This teaching is idealistic, and none of us has been able to live up to it completely, but it is not crazy or deranged:

> Then Judas (not Judas Iscariot) said, 'But, Lord, why do you intend to show yourself to us and not to the world?'
>
> Jesus replied, 'Anyone who loves me will obey my teaching. My Father will love them, and we will come to them and make our home with them . . . Peace I leave with you; my peace I give you.'
> (John 14:22–23, 27)

Authority, based on love, leads to peace, not to disorder.

Relationship based on love

Everything that Jesus taught about relationship – with God, with one another – was based on love (see chapter 4). The kingdom of God is based on relationship, and all of his people 'have instant, immediate, direct and valued access into the very presence of the living God'.[8] Our relationship with one another is based on our love for Jesus, and God the Father loves us. Our love is based on belief, and it results in peace

(John 16:27, 31, 33). John emphasizes this triangular relationship – between God the Father, Jesus and his followers – and it is all based on love (John 17:9–19). This network of relationships is complex, spiritual and not easily subject to mental or physical examination, but it is certainly not mad.

Jesus' generous love is for everyone, and especially towards the poor, the distressed, the despised, and, in the patriarchal society in which he lived, women. This is revealed in the story of the woman who washed Jesus' feet. She was a 'woman in that town who lived a sinful life'. Jesus' conclusion is that 'her many sins have been forgiven – as her great love has shown' (Luke 7:37, 47). In all healthy relationships, love is central and 'God is love' (1 John 4:8). (This is developed further in chapter 6.)

Because of his huge significance for individuals and his impact on history, Jesus' detractors dubbed him insane. Is this claim legitimate? Was he insane, or at least mentally deranged? Were Jesus' words and teaching meaningless? We will look at mental illness in more detail – each condition is not arbitrary, but shows a range of different patterns.

We believe Jesus was trustworthy: he taught with authority, and his authority came from God. Much of his teaching concerned healthy relationships between individuals and with God: 'God is love.' Following the logic of the 'trilemma', if we, as psychiatrists, can successfully prove that Jesus was not mentally deranged, then any critic has to prove that Jesus was a bad man unless he or she recognizes him as God.

Could the Master who washed the feet of his followers (John 13:5) be other than a good and humble man?

2. THE TEST OF PSYCHOSIS: 'OUT OF HIS MIND'

It is frequently said that if Christ came to the world now
he would once again be crucified. This is not entirely true.
The world has changed; it is more immersed
in 'understanding.' Therefore Christ would
be ridiculed, treated as a mad man,
but a mad man at whom one laughs.
Søren Kierkegaard

Psychosis has specific features which we will consider in this chapter. Did Jesus suffer from what we might now describe as psychosis? Some people declare Jesus to be mad, and psychosis may be akin to what they are implying. Also, we discuss how some of Jesus' teaching and actions may not be understood, and therefore considered psychotic from a modern perspective. In the last chapter we looked in more general terms at Jesus and mental illness, but now we will focus on the accusation that he was overtly mad.

Jesus' disciples clearly did not think of him as mentally ill, and he did not think that way about himself either. There was no indication that his followers felt that they should care for or protect him, nor that he expected this from them.

One of his many claims for himself was: 'I am the way and the truth and the life' (John 14:6). Jesus said this with conviction, and his disciples believed him. Taken out of context, it sounds megalomaniac, but if true, it is still valid today.

Was he a maniac, or was it true?

Reaction of family and experts

It is difficult to work out how our present-day assumptions and prejudices about madness and mental illness fit into first-century thinking in Palestine. 'Illness of the mind' is a Renaissance concept, which would have been quite foreign to the people among whom Jesus lived. Psychiatry, as a defined discipline within medicine, only dates from about 1800. So in the Bible there are accounts of people who seem mad – for example, Nebuchadnezzar (Daniel 4:31–33) – but there is no reference to mental illness as such.

There were people in the Gospels who, from our viewpoint nowadays, suffered from mental illness and were regarded as insane. Within their own culture it had to be possible to describe this, explain it and deal with it appropriately. Then, as now, a person who was mad could not take responsibility for his or her actions, and others had to take charge.

Mark's Gospel gives a vivid account of the hectic pace of Jesus' ministry on one occasion. Jesus first had to answer criticism from the Pharisees, and from John the Baptist's disciples, about fasting. Then he taught that 'the Sabbath was made for man, not man for the Sabbath' (Mark 2:27), before healing a man with a withered hand on the Sabbath day, which was seen as both wonderful and disgraceful. The crowds following Jesus' every word and action had become enormous, and criticism by the Pharisees had progressed from hostility and disapproval to plotting against his life. Pressure was mounting day by day.

Then we read that Jesus entered a house and the crowds became so dense that he and his disciples could not eat. 'When his family heard about this, they went to take charge of him, for they said, "He is out of his mind"' (Mark 3:21). A modern paraphrase helps us grasp the background better: 'Jesus came home and, as usual, a crowd gathered – so many making demands on him that that there wasn't even time to eat' (MSG).

If we carefully consider the preceding events, the reaction of Jesus' family is not so surprising. He had left home and given up a good job as a carpenter to become a homeless itinerant preacher, besides which, he had started a 'peculiar society' with the most diverse individuals – not a very normal group. Also, he had placed himself in imminent danger with the authorities because of his strange teaching. And now he was under so much pressure from people's demands that 'set mealtimes were impossible. This, to them, was the last straw . . . so they decided that they must save Jesus from the consequences of his own vocation.'[1] They had not understood the purpose at all, nor the quality and the drive of Jesus' work. So they concluded that he must be 'out of his mind' – a normal man would not do the kind of things he does – and that he needed to be protected from himself.

Jesus was in the district of Galilee at the time, and a group of experts in the religious law who had come down from Jerusalem (several days' journey away) became involved and said, 'He is possessed by Beelzebul! By the prince of demons he is driving out demons' (Mark 3:22). Jesus countered this with the argument: 'How can Satan drive out Satan?' (Mark 3:23), and told them a parable of how a kingdom divided against itself could not survive. The family had said he was mad; the teachers of the law rephrased this within their worldview and claimed that he was possessed by Beelzebul; and both, for different reasons, considered that he should be restrained and silenced.

On another occasion Jesus was teaching his hearers about the good shepherd looking after, and even laying down his life for, his sheep, a picture that would have been well recognized by his audience, from their reading of the Old Testament, as referring to God, the shepherd, and his sheep, the people of Israel (Ezekiel 34). Jesus says to them, 'I am the good shepherd; I know my sheep and my sheep know me . . . and I lay down my life for the sheep' (John 10:14, 15). He goes on to say, 'I have other sheep that are not of this sheepfold. I must bring them also. They too will listen to my voice, and there shall be one flock and one shepherd' (John 10:16). Those 'other sheep', not in the sheepfold of Israel, included the vast throng of followers of Christ who are not Jewish. This made the Jewish leaders very angry:

> Many of them said, 'He is demon-possessed and raving mad. Why listen to him?'
> But others said, 'These are not the sayings of a man possessed by a demon. Can a demon open the eyes of the blind?'
> (John 10:20–21)

They recognized that either what Jesus said about coming from God must be true or he was mad – or evil, demon-possessed. They appreciated then what we must realize now. He was not just a wise teacher giving good, sensible moral advice, nor an itinerant healer, but his claims about himself were revolutionary, upsetting the whole social and religious order: they were either true, or he had to be mad or evil.

But was he the Messiah, sent by God to save the world?

Listen to the enigmatic conversation between Jesus and Pilate at his trial (which we come back to in chapter 7). 'Are you the king of the Jews?' Pilate asked Jesus. In answer, Jesus said, 'My kingdom is not of this world. If it were, my servants would fight to prevent my arrest by the Jewish leaders. But now my kingdom is from another place' (John 18:33, 36). In Pilate's cynical eyes, those of a wary military governor of an occupying force, Jesus was obviously not a king, beaten and bedraggled as he was before him, but was he dangerous? Pilate did not appear to understand what Jesus was saying, but he was not a threat, and so he must be a harmless madman. Throughout his life when people could not understand Jesus, or did not want to take the trouble to do so, they declared him insane. In today's terms, what Jesus said and did was counter-cultural, so the pillars of society decreed he must be mad. But what is 'mad'?

Patterns of psychotic illness

To describe someone as mad, crazy or insane may either be an attempt at an accurate description of his or her mental state or, more likely, a means of discrediting what that person says or does. Psychiatrists are reluctant to categorize people with any of these words; they use the term 'psychosis'. This is not stigmatizing to the same extent, and lends more precision to the description. Until one names or categorizes a problem (that is, diagnosis), one cannot start to solve it. We may describe a person suffering from 'psychosis' as being 'out of touch with reality'. Someone who is severely depressed or acutely anxious is well aware of reality, and cannot cope with it; someone with a schizophrenic illness may not be aware of what is taking place outside himself or herself. Lack of insight is characteristic of psychotic illness and entails a failure to accept that one is ill and to appreciate that the symptoms are due to illness.[2]

A middle-aged woman became abusive to her neighbours and threatened complete strangers in the street with a kettle of boiling water. In desperation, her husband arranged for a psychiatrist to visit her. When he arrived, she tried to convince him that it was her husband who was mad and should be taken into care. She was out of touch with reality and lacking insight.

As we have already said, 'mental illness' is not random or without form, but different mental illnesses show distinct patterns of symptoms in speech and behaviour. We try to diagnose by finding the personal meaning for sufferers, understanding their internal state through empathy, and distinguishing between the form of their illness and the content of their experience. Groups of symptoms sometimes occur together, and these are described as 'syndromes'. These patterns are relatively constant and allow the psychiatrist to make a diagnosis with a fair degree of accuracy. For example, learning disability (intellectual disability) presents quite differently from schizophrenia. Difficulty in diagnosis comes with borderline and mixed presentations of symptoms.

When Philip started harrassing shoppers in a city street with bizarre threats and insisting that foreign battleships were coming down the high street, the police took him to a psychiatric unit. He came under the care of a consultant psychiatrist for a few years afterwards. Philip believed that this doctor was controlling his thoughts – taking some thoughts out of his head and putting others in. When he saw a complicated radiological instrument in the hospital, he knew, with complete certainty, that this was a machine for controlling his thoughts. He heard low, threatening voices with Eastern

European accents talking about him in derogatory terms and making disparaging remarks about his puny body. Philip suffered from paranoid schizophrenia and was treated for many years, mostly at home with regular visits from a community psychiatric nurse. Occasionally he became more disturbed and had to be readmitted.

As well as schizophrenia, the other major group of conditions that may result in psychosis are 'mood disorders', both mania and depression. Psychosis represents the extreme level of severity at both ends of the mood spectrum. Psychotic depression is incompatible with the normal demands of everyday life; the sufferer may be mute and inert. 'Psychotic states of mania are characterized by greater pressure of speech, more open hostility, severe agitation, no need for sleep, flight of thoughts, severe distractibility and grandiose delusions.'[3] Coming back to our subject, Jesus never showed anything remotely similar to either depressive or manic psychosis.

Features of psychotic illness

What are the distinct features of psychotic illnesses, making them different from other mental illnesses? We have already mentioned lack of contact with reality and a loss of insight. Also prominent are delusions, hallucinations and thought disorder, which we have already mentioned. A delusion is an idea or belief expressed with unusual persistence or force, not shared by others in the local community and exerting an undue influence on the person's life.[4] Hallucination is a false perception – hearing, seeing, feeling, tasting, smelling – which occurs alongside real perceptions. Highly significant, especially in schizophrenia, are auditory hallucinations, among which 'hearing voices' is frequent. Thought disorder may be revealed in the patient's subjective awareness of his or her own disturbed thinking patterns, and the manifestation of abnormal thinking betrayed in his or her speech.[5]

In the account of the wild man, Legion, and the Gerasene swine in Luke's Gospel, there is nothing to prove that the man was suffering from schizophrenia (Luke 8:26–39). We are told that he was, in our terminology, mentally disturbed, and that he was possessed by a legion of demons. For a present-day psychiatrist, the diagnosis is unknown, but he appeared to suffer from a psychotic illness.

Schizophrenia is the most frequently experienced condition causing psychotic thinking and behaviour. It often starts in early adult life and may last for many years or even decades. The features are often listed as 'positive' symptoms – delusion, hallucination, thought disorder, which we have already mentioned – and 'negative' symptoms, which are often more difficult to describe and ascertain, but cause enormous long-term disability in leading a normal life. The negative symptoms of schizophrenia result in severe social disability – at home with relatives, in being able to work, and difficulties in other situations such as church. They include a flattening of affect, poverty of speech and loss of drive. They are largely responsible for the extreme difficulty in the rehabilitation of those with long-term illness, causing problems with relationships, and a loss of motivation to initiate any constructive activity.

During Martin's first year reading mathematics at Oxford University, he became acutely mentally ill and had to withdraw from the course. At home and in hospital he was treated for several years for schizophrenia, but was eventually stable enough to complete his degree at another university. Twenty years later, he was a genial, harmless middle-aged man with no obvious delusions, hallucinations or thought disorder, but unfortunately he had no initiative or drive. He lived in sheltered accommodation and made no deep or lasting relationships with others. Although positive symptoms of schizophrenia had cleared, he still suffered from the long-term effects of negative symptoms.

Did Jesus experience symptoms of psychotic illness?

Now we have seen the patterns of symptoms and signs, the 'syndromes', for the different conditions that are described as 'psychosis'. They do not add up to some sort of non-specific 'craziness', but to precise and definite psychiatric disorders, quite different from others in terms of cause, onset, course and outcome.

Did Jesus show any of these signs and symptoms? With reference to the three-year course of his ministry, the only psychotic conditions that could possibly be considered are schizophrenia, and mania, as part of bipolar disorder. The story of his life, as presented in the Gospels, is so far from any description of mania as to make it inconceivable. There is no evidence in his speech or behaviour of a flight of ideas or overactivity, and his claims about himself were based on Scripture rather than grandiosity.

Delusion

We know that Jesus did make some astonishing statements – they amazed people at the time, and those who take them seriously now continue to be surprised. But was he deluded?

Delusion has been defined as 'a false, unshakeable idea or belief, which is out of keeping with the patient's educational, cultural and social background and held with extraordinary conviction and subjective certainty'.[6] Did Jesus fulfil these criteria in what he said? Whether the ideas he expressed are regarded as true or false depends upon the perspective of the commentator – Christians believe that what he said was true. He maintained what he said with conviction, up to and including his death from crucifixion. His claims are directly traceable to many references in the Old Testament, especially the Psalms and prophets, about the coming Messiah, the King, the Suffering Servant and the Saviour of the world. Jesus' beliefs were held with conviction and certainty, but the other essential requirements for 'delusion' are not fulfilled.

Jesus said to his critics, 'You are from below; I am from above. You are of this world; I am not of this world' (John 8:23). If this were stated by a patient on a psychiatric ward, it might be regarded as a mad thing to say, particularly if it were not backed up by appropriate action, but Jesus must be taken in context. His words formed part of a longer debate with the Pharisees who were trying to demolish his arguments. What he said arose from his beliefs, developed throughout his life, that he was here, on earth, to do his Father's will. He understood that his work arose directly from his knowledge of the Scriptures, and these he applied.

On seven occasions in the Gospel of John, Jesus is recorded as saying, 'I am . . .' (In chapter 9 we will consider who Jesus claimed to be, and the challenge for us: who do we say he is?) Each one of these 'I ams', taken out of context, was breathtaking self-aggrandizement, and could imply delusion to the critical reader. However, taken in context, these sayings show a great coherence with his work, and they are an expression of mental lucidity, not insanity.

Jesus' followers became increasingly explicit throughout his public ministry that he was the Messiah. This realization resulted in a noisy crowd at his triumphal entry into Jerusalem a week before he died. They shouted, 'Hosanna! Blessed is he who comes in the name of the Lord! Blessed is the coming kingdom of our father David! Hosanna in the highest heaven!' (Mark 11:9–10).

Jesus believed that he was the Messiah: he would bring in God's kingdom, he would suffer, die and be raised again, and he would save the world. This was not delusion, but a consistently held belief about his destiny. Delusion brings restriction in thinking – a single, often simple, dominant notion such as 'the aliens are going to harm me' – while in Jesus' 'I am' statements there is huge richness of content. This layered structure and variety cannot be delusional.

Hallucination

Hallucination is, in its simplest definition, a perception without an object,[7] that is, seeing, hearing and so on, without there being anything to be seen or heard. It is often a sign of mental illness.

Did Jesus ever suffer from hallucination? We do not think so. There are accounts of Jesus' temptation by the devil in the wilderness in the Gospels of Matthew (4:1–11), Mark (1:12–13) and Luke (4:1–13). There is no description of Jesus' perception during the temptations – we simply read that the devil 'said to him', 'took him', but in what manner we know not. Despite the vivid imagery of Renaissance artists, we are not told how the temptations took place; Tom Wright describes it thus: 'the devil's voice appears as a string of natural ideas in his own head.'[8] For the experience described to be regarded as hallucination, it would have to be a 'perception', that is, experienced as a sensation of sight, hearing and so on. We are not given such a description, and so we cannot go beyond saying that it was a 'vision', with the precise nature of the subjective experience unknown. Hallucination could imply psychosis, but this was not Jesus' experience. The account of his temptations in the three Gospels is telling us about Jesus' spiritual state undergoing temptation, not his mental state. On the other hand, we discover a striking lucidity in the answers Jesus gave to each of the temptations. His sharpness, enabling him to quote appropriate texts of Scripture, and the coherence of his arguments, make a brilliant defence against the devil's assault. All of this is very far from the mental state of psychosis.

In the accounts of the transfiguration of Jesus, whatever the perception of the three apostles who climbed the mountain with him, there is nothing to suggest that Jesus experienced either visual or auditory hallucinations.[9] There is no comment in any of the three Gospels on Jesus' perception at the time – seeing or hearing – only his speech is recorded. Were the post-resurrection appearances of Jesus to his followers hallucinations? No, because the same perception was held by many different people. Hallucination is an individual, not a shared, phenomenon.

Thought disorder

Many people, including Jesus' disciples, had difficulty in understanding some of his sayings. As we pointed out earlier, we still find some of what he said problematic today. That is not because his teachings were confused or incomprehensible, as in the 'formal thought disorder' of psychosis, but rather because his thoughts and speech were on a different plane from ours – spiritual, and showing his constant contact with God.

Schizophrenic or formal thought disorder is an alteration from normal thinking that the sufferer describes subjectively regarding the thinking process. One sufferer described it thus: 'My thoughts are being pushed into the upper left corner of my brain.' There are some quite specific faults in the thinking process and consequent speech produced. Two of these, particularly characteristic of schizophrenia, taken almost at random, are derailment and thought withdrawal. Derailment implies a loosening of association so that ideas slip on to either an obliquely related, or totally unrelated, theme. For example, 'The traffic is rumbling along the main road. They are going to the north. Why do girls always play pantomime heroes?'[10] Thought withdrawal was once described thus: 'My thinking stopped because the thoughts were suddenly taken out of my head.' These abnormalities would be noticed by a trained listener, but would be unlikely to be recorded and written down unless with the intention of demonstrating the disorder. There is no hint or suggestion of thought disorder in any Gospel record of Jesus' sayings.

Jesus used such expressions as 'eat my flesh' and 'drink my blood' (John 6:53–55), and many thoughtless critics throughout the ages have taken that literally, and accused Christians of cannibalism. But like all Jesus' sayings, it must be taken in context. We will discuss 'concreteness of thought and expression' later in this chapter. There is no evidence that Jesus ever showed the negative symptoms of thought disorder: affective flattening, poverty of speech or loss of drive.

In the life and sayings of Jesus there is nothing to suggest that he suffered from delusions, hallucinations or thought disorder. The more carefully we look, the less we find. Close examination of the Gospels reveals no trace of psychosis.

So why have people made such claims?

Possibilities for misunderstanding

Words, and their use, may result in misunderstanding, especially in the realm of religion. There can be a spurious similarity between how believers describe the everyday aspects of their spiritual life and what secular people would see as strange or even mad. When we look at Jesus with our twenty-first-century eyes, some actions that were not seen as mad at the time may be seen as psychotic now.

Prayer seems to be a pointless activity to many people, and if someone else believes in the power of prayer, that to them is inexplicable and crazy. Jesus prayed, and it was a source of authority and strength in his life. We even know about the content of some of his prayer – praise to God and for knowing him for himself; through prayer he had constant and direct contact with his Father (Matthew 11:25–30). It was essential, central to his ministry. Prayer may be incomprehensible to non-believers because they cannot see that it is 'real', that there is communication between the believer and God. Therefore, they think that it must be delusional – false belief, hallucinatory – a false perception or thought disordered. Jesus understood our difficulties with prayer. He wants our prayers to be real and conversational with God: 'When you pray, do not keep on babbling like pagans . . . your Father knows what you need before you ask him' (Matthew 6:7–8). Our prayers, and Jesus' prayers, are not delusional acts.

Unbelievers assume that it is impossible to 'hear the voice of God' – there must be another, mentally disordered, explanation. Yet 'hearing the voice of God' is described as a frequent experience within some churches, and many more believe that they have been helped by God directly in their lives in answer to their prayers.

Jesus, in the account of his temptation in the wilderness, experienced the devil trying to lead him astray (Luke 4:1–13). There is nothing to suggest hallucination: the real action was going on inside Jesus' mind. Through this experience Jesus confirmed to himself that he must fulfil his destiny and do his Father's will. The experiences described were not perceptions, and therefore do not meet the criteria required for 'hallucination'.

Jesus prayed aloud, for example, in the garden of Gethsemane (Mark 14:36). Speaking to God makes perfect sense when we know that Jesus believed 'his Father' was there and ready to hear him at any moment of the day.

Many Christians use such expressions as 'being in Christ', 'Christ in me', 'that he (Jesus) may live in us and we in him'.[11] Such people are not mentally deranged; theirs is a spiritual experience and completely different from mental illness. It is an internal experience, of God being inside, helping, facilitating the person to be more truly who he or she is, wants to be and act; it is quite unlike any form of mental illness.[12] These expressions, when used by a mentally healthy believer, are not to be taken concretely – in which organ of the body is Christ located?

Concreteness and reality

This psychotic experience of 'concreteness' is a useful handle to open the door on the dilemma of literal/spiritual, actual/metaphorical. In our science- and technology-based culture, there is a tendency to see only the literal/physical as real and powerful, and the spiritual/metaphorical as neither of these. Jesus teaches against this. Often he encourages his hearers to think about matters of the spirit: 'God is spirit, and his worshippers must worship in the Spirit and in truth' (John 4:24). There was no possibility for metaphor in the thinking of someone suffering from schizophrenia who had interpreted Scripture literally and tried to remove his own eye.

Christians make a distinction between metaphor – 'the lamb of God' – and the physical – the historical person of Jesus, his death on the cross and his resurrection. The kingdom that Jesus spoke about to Pilate was real, but, at that time, spiritual and not physical. Pilate would have been thinking about another kingdom, like Herod's in Galilee – puppet, ephemeral, but literal. Jesus was talking about the kingdom, now in the minds and souls of his followers and believers, but eventually to spread right round the world. Which was more powerful? Today Herod is long gone and, except through the story of Jesus, forgotten; the kingdom of God has grown over the past 2,000 years and is still growing throughout the world.

In our society the word 'paranoid' is used frequently, and loosely. In psychiatry, the term implies ideas or beliefs of self-reference – thinking that the voice on the radio talking about oil wells in Azerbaijan, for example, refers to me. In practice, these self-referent ideas are usually persecutory: the idea, without supporting evidence, that 'everyone wants to be helpful to me' is not commonly presented to a psychiatrist!

Jesus predicted his own suffering, rejection, crucifixion and resurrection (Luke 9:22). Was this a paranoid idea? No, not in a psychiatric sense; it was an idea of self-reference, but also it was literally true for his future, foretelling what would happen in fulfilling his vocation to save the world. Was he 'psychic' to know this? No, Jesus knew in detail the Old Testament Scriptures about the 'suffering servant', and he knew that these applied to him (Isaiah 52:13 – 53:12). That he would suffer and die and bear the sins of many was foretold, and that he would rise again. Throughout his life he followed a single plan. A depressive delusion that 'I ought to be killed' can lead to putting oneself in the way of being killed. Jesus' actions were not like that: he was not suicidal in the sense of acting so as to be killed on the basis of delusion. He was always concordant with his longstanding teaching about his mission and his understanding of Scripture.

Again, a few days before he was crucified, Jesus said, 'If the world hates you, keep in mind that it hated me first' (John 15:18). Jesus was not paranoid in any pathological sense: this was not a persecutory delusion, but rather a statement of fact. Jesus goes on to say that his followers are 'not of this world', and that the Holy Spirit will be sent to help them.

Sometimes believers, in their prayers, ask God to take control of their lives. What do they mean, and does he do so? This is a request not that Christ should control me against my will, but rather that he is alongside and inside, helping and encouraging me to be more my true self, myself as I would like to be.[13] This is quite different from the 'delusions of control' that sometimes feature in schizophrenia.

So why do people say that Jesus must have been mad?

The arguments for Jesus suffering from madness or psychosis seem pretty threadbare. So why do people even now say that Jesus must have been mad?

A very superficial reading of the accounts of Jesus' life in a twenty-first-century context, with no explanations put forward for his surprising and almost outrageous sayings, might lead the reader to dismiss Jesus, and what he said, as mad. What Jesus said is inexplicable to someone who cannot think beyond the physical and mechanistic; therefore, the superficial reader claims, it must be mad.

But beyond these arguments, Jesus' teaching is often challenging, uncompromising and uncomfortable. How can he be discredited more effectively than by contending that his words are the outpouring of a madman, and can therefore be ignored? People now want to say that he is mad so that he can be banished from normal society and locked away in an asylum, both literally and metaphorically, well away from everyday life – a madman 'at whom one laughs' (Søren Kierkegaard) and whom one ignores.

Jesus did not suffer from a psychotic illness. There is nothing to substantiate a claim of delusion, hallucination, thought disorder or any other indicator. 'Madness' has been excluded, but is there a possibility that Jesus suffered from any other mental illness? This we will explore further now.

3. THE TEST OF MENTAL IMPAIRMENT: 'A MAN OF SORROWS'

A man of sorrows and acquainted with grief.
Isaiah 53:3, KJV

In chapter 2 we argued from psychiatric principles that Jesus was not overtly 'mad' or psychotic. That, however, is only the first part of the argument. There is a vast difference between someone suffering a psychotic illness, perhaps an in-patient on a psychiatric ward or the unfortunate King George III, and a person enduring profound but less dramatic mental illness while trying to carry on with normal life. Somebody might well go on to say about the latter, 'All right, he was not mad, but he was seriously mentally ill and therefore unfit for our complete trust.'

Other mental illnesses

Does it really matter whether Jesus suffered from mental illness? Peter, a soldier, had been subjected to life-threatening, prolonged stress. In Afghanistan he had been on a difficult and responsible tour of duty and was then a victim in a bomb attack. Now he had gloomy and suicidal thoughts; depression and extreme anxiety had made him unable to work. Pam, his long-suffering wife, found him unpredictable and difficult to live with, but she coped: 'He is ill; I just have to accept that and hope that he will get better.' Peter's condition had resulted in the impairment of his judgment in many ways, and this was recognized by other people. Similarly, Jesus was subjected to long-term enmity and then suffered catastrophic torture resulting in his death. However, there is no record, in his case, of depression, anxiety or impairment of judgment, and this is an important consideration, following the argument in chapter 1 about trusting Jesus. If we are to continue to trust Jesus, then we need to feel that he is not impaired by mental disorder.

Amelia, who suffered from anorexia nervosa, shared a student flat. Her flatmate, Fatima, discovered that she had stolen her breakfast cereal. She did not accuse her because she realized that 'she is ill and I must make allowances'. But we would not want any 'allowances' to have to be made for Jesus. If Jesus' judgment were impaired, there would be much more at stake: grounds for not trusting or believing him.

Neither Peter nor Amelia would be considered 'mad' or psychotic, as described in chapter 2, but both suffered from mental illness that meant that their friends and relations, the military and the university authorities and those caring for them, had to 'make allowances'. While they were ill, neither of them was able to take full responsibility: in that sense they were not fully trustworthy.

Normal human emotions

Jesus was wholly and fully human. He grew and developed normally; he ate and drank; he walked long distances; he suffered pain and died. And he experienced a wide range of emotions, appropriate in direction and level within the context in which they occurred.

He was a real man, not an appearance of man.[1] He wept; he knew great sadness. Tom Wright puts it like this: 'When we look at Jesus, *not least when we look at Jesus in tears,* we are seeing not just a flesh-and-blood human being but the Word made flesh.'[2] 'The Word became flesh and made his dwelling among us' (John 1:14) implies that Jesus became human in all respects, including his emotions. So Jesus wept (John 11:35), over Lazarus and for Lazarus's sisters' distress.

He could, and did, become angry. He overturned tables in the temple (Matthew 21:12), and was incensed – justifiably. He became indignant with the disciples who tried to prevent children from being brought to him: 'Let the little children come to me, and do not hinder them, for the kingdom of God belongs to such as these' (Mark 10:14).

He looked on the rich young ruler and 'loved him' (Mark 10:21). There are five references in John's Gospel to 'the disciple whom Jesus loved'.[3] He had keen sympathy for suffering individuals, and for a crowd: 'When he saw the crowds, he had compassion on them, because they were harassed and helpless, like sheep without a shepherd' (Matthew 9:36).

Jesus was misunderstood, sometimes even by his own disciples, and this resulted in his being profoundly alone as he went into his arrest, trial and crucifixion (Luke 22:24–38). This loneliness did not come from mental illness or abnormality of personality, but because of the message he was carrying and what he was doing about it.

His 'soul was troubled' (John 12:27), but he did not ask his Father to save him, because 'it was for this very reason I came to this hour'. Jesus is described as being 'troubled in spirit' (John 13:21), but he always deals with unpleasant emotion without neurosis or emotional disturbance. We read, 'My soul is overwhelmed with sorrow to the point of death' (Matthew 26:38). His grief and misery were extreme, but they arose from circumstances, not illness. There is no description of excessive, or inadequate, emotional reaction, nor is there evidence of emotion being directed towards an inappropriate recipient. Taken in context, not even 'love your enemies' (Matthew 5:44) is emotionally inappropriate. He was no robot without emotion – he really did suffer, but his judgment was never impaired by unpleasant emotions.

Jesus was, throughout his earthly life, a happy person. He certainly had times of darkness, grief and sorrow, but most of the time he was optimistic and cheerful. There are accounts, often very brief, of Jesus experiencing a wide range of varying emotions. These were attuned to the different circumstances in which he found himself and the people with whom he interacted.

Depression and anxiety
Depressive disorder and anxiety disorder are the most commonly occurring mental illnesses. Did Jesus suffer from either of these?

Depression is the mood associated with experience of loss. 'Losses' include that of a person, of a limb, of home, and other losses too. A mental process takes place in which the person is 'making real inside the self, events which have already occurred in reality outside'.[4] In depression, grief is experienced, and sometimes feelings of helplessness and hopelessness too.[5] Jesus suffered massive losses, starting with loss of his heavenly home for a season and culminating in his death by crucifixion. Throughout his career he anticipated these losses, knowing that they would happen, but he never demonstrated depression (see chapter 7).

Depressive illness may occur as an episode in bipolar disorder. People with bipolar disorder usually have periods of depression and also episodes of grandiose ideas, excessive activity, elation and irritability. Did Jesus show excessive mood swings? There is no evidence of overactivity or 'flight of ideas'. In fact, what is supremely apparent in the life of Jesus is his calm tranquility in the midst of vast crowds and a superhuman workload. His peace is the *antithesis* of mania.

How about Jesus' breathtaking claims for himself as a king, for example, to Pilate (Matthew 27:11), riding a donkey into Jerusalem with the adulation of the crowd (Matthew 21), and what he said to his disciples? Were these grandiose ideas? There is a tradition throughout the Psalms and Old Testament prophets that God himself would be King on earth and reign in justice: the Messiah, in the line of David, would rule over Israel. Jesus fulfils these claims. He was not fraudulent or megalomaniac; he predicted for himself the fulfilment of these prophecies, including an ignominious death.

Anxiety has been described as the fear of loss. When we are faced with real threat or danger, anxiety is often appropriate and may even be life saving. When a man walking across a field realizes that he shares it with an angry bull, he becomes anxious and this accelerates his escape. If, six months later, he still feels so anxious that he cannot go to work, this has become pathological. The major provocations for anxiety are fear of separation and fear of the unknown, or danger. There was plenty of opportunity in Jesus' life to experience these fears. He was exposed to many threatening circumstances, but his reaction was always calm, and on many occasions he said, 'Fear not!' Even in his final week, he showed no anxiety and continued to trust his Father absolutely.

Jesus taught about anxiety: 'Do not worry about . . .' (Matthew 6:25–34). He then goes on with a list of things that should not cause us concern. He is not teaching about anxiety disorder or 'free-floating anxiety'; anxiety state is quite different from preoccupation with material concerns about such matters as clothes, food and physical appearance. He wanted people to relinquish anxiety about material things: 'the worries of this life and the deceitfulness of wealth' that prevent us from trusting God (Matthew 13:22). He is condemning not anxiety disorder, but the attitude of being taken up with this world's concerns to the exclusion of God.

In his teaching Jesus seems to anticipate cognitive therapy for anxiety. This type of treatment is based on the assumption that it is not events themselves, but people's expectations of events that produce negative emotion such as anxiety. Patients with anxiety disorder systematically overestimate danger, and treatment aims to help them identify negative, danger-related thoughts and beliefs and to modify these 'cognitions' and the processes that maintain them.[6] Sufferers are encouraged to set up an internal argument inside their mind to challenge their cognitions, and as they succeed in this, so symptoms further diminish. Christopher Williams and co-authors of *I'm Not Supposed to Feel Like This*[7] describe the application of these principles for the treatment of Christians suffering from depression and anxiety. Jesus encourages us not to worry about what we will eat, drink, wear, 'because your heavenly Father knows that you need them' (Matthew 6:32); he challenges our cognitions. Jesus showed no evidence of anxiety himself, but it must have been widely prevalent in an occupied land.

Mental symptoms include depressed mood, morbid elation and overactivity, inappropriate or prolonged anxiety, guilt feelings, unwanted fear, despair and despondency, gloom and moodiness, and physical symptoms of psychological origin. None of the accounts of Jesus' feelings, sayings and actions describes any of these symptoms. Not only was Jesus free from the symptoms of mental illness, but he brought peace into the lives of those whom he met, and hope rather than despair.

No mental symptoms

To be regarded as a symptom of mental illness, an experience must be unpleasant, prolonged, excessive and hindering a normal life. Following bereavement of a loved one, anyone will be very unhappy; that is not depression. If, however, a person is miserable and feeling suicidal for more than a year after quarrelling with a friend, then the possibility of depressive illness should be borne in mind. Symptoms may occur with emotions, such as depression or anxiety, in thinking, such as poor memory or difficulty with calculation, or in the capacity to exert the will or make decisions. None of these symptoms is described in the writings about Jesus. His intellectual capacity and memory have never been doubted, nor has his capacity for decisive action (see chapter 5).

Believers, and others, frequently admit to feelings of guilt. Sometimes, however, inappropriate feelings of guilt occur as a psychiatric symptom, for example, in depressive illness. Guilt is not described in the accounts of Jesus because 'he committed no sin' (1 Peter 2:22), and he had feelings of sympathy, but not guilt, for the misfortunes of others. Even in his final week he had compassion for others, but no feeling of guilt. From the cross, far from feeling that he had failed in his life's work, he exclaimed in a loud voice, 'It is finished!' (John 19:30, NKJV). His life's work was completed. (This is developed further in chapter 7.)

Some disturbance in relationship occurs in all mental illnesses. We describe Jesus' relationships in more detail in chapter 6, but for now we will assert that at no time did he show an inability to relate suitably. Whereas having problems relating to others occurs with 'neurosis', Jesus' relationships were uncomplicated by doubts about himself. Jesus' life was an example to his followers, and the key to his relationships was love: 'I have set you an example that you should do as I have done for you' (John 13:15).

Jesus did not display the distortion in self-image and the way one regards oneself in relation to the world that occurs in mental illness. He is the very opposite of the power-craving neurotic.

Characteristic of psychological disturbance in thinking about oneself is 'the tyranny of inevitability' – sufferers feel that whatever they try to do, they cannot alter the world they live in: there's an external 'locus of control'[8] – their life and actions are entirely at the whim of outside circumstances. This occurs in neurosis and depression. But Jesus controlled his own actions and destiny, even to the extent of foretelling and accepting his own death by crucifixion, and resurrection (Matthew 16:21, 24).

Jesus functioned well in his work and relationships. He displayed no loss of energy, initiative or drive. We saw how he was aware throughout his public ministry that he was fulfilling his destiny, foretold in the Old Testament. This explains much of what might otherwise be called neurotic, self-destructive, negative behaviour, for example, his accept-ance of a death sentence by Pontius Pilate. Jesus died instead of Barabbas, to fulfil the prophecy: ' "he was numbered with the transgressors"; and I tell you that this must be fulfilled in me' (Luke 22:37). This was a quotation from the book of Isaiah (Isaiah 52:13 – 53:12). Jesus' actions were deliberate and in obedience to his calling.

Jesus remained asleep in a boat through a raging storm that frightened even seasoned fishermen. This does not reveal much background anxiety in his make-up (Matthew 8:23–25)! Why was he so peaceful? The clue comes in his ability to calm the storm: he was in constant contact with God, his Father, who controlled the storm. His rejoinder to the frightened disciples was: 'Why are you so afraid? Do you still have no faith?' (Mark 4:40). He was not an anxious person – the very opposite of anxiety-prone; he had total faith in God.

Jesus was not anxious because he was able to accept what he had been given, by his Father, for each day. He always showed compassion towards those who were suffering. Concerning fear, we saw earlier that Jesus preached not against fear as a pathological emotion, but against fear that demonstrates lack of trust. When Peter responds to Jesus' invitation and walks on the water, he looks at the raging seas, fear replaces trust and he starts to sink (Matthew 14:29–30).

So Jesus is not exhorting fragile, fearful, chronically anxious people to 'stop worrying', as many thoughtless people do today, nor commenting on anxiety disorder as a pathological condition. He is preaching against the rich, scheming and hoarding, who deny the place of God in their lives in order to be richer. Jesus experienced the provocations for both depressive illness and anxiety disorder, but he did not suffer from either condition, nor did he show the mood swings of bipolar disorder.

Were there any other psychiatric conditions?

We have now considered psychotic disorders (chapter 2), the frequent conditions of depressive illness and anxiety state, and found that there is no evidence for Jesus having suffered from any of them. But did he suffer from another psychiatric illness? Jesus was once described as a 'wine bibber'. This was deliberately hostile towards Jesus: 'The Son of man came eating and drinking, and they say, "Behold a man gluttonous, and a winebibber, a friend of publicans and sinners"' (Matthew 11:19, KJV). But he was not alcoholic, and the accusation itself was a backhanded compliment: Jesus believed that his ministry was to sinners, and, in keeping with this, he did indeed socialize and eat with them.

Obsessive disorder

Jesus showed no trace of obsessive disorder: in the area of cleanliness, taken to extremes by the Pharisees, his disciples ate food without washing, and he did not correct them (Mark 7:1–13); he taught rather about being 'clean' in heart and behaviour (Mark 7:14–23). He was not legalistic: we should honour God rather than man-made traditions was the emphasis. In keeping the Sabbath, Jesus was in no way obsessional: there was no controlling scrupulosity in instructing his followers how to keep the Sabbath. 'The Son of Man is Lord of the Sabbath,' he said (Luke 6:5). He did not feel that he was controlled by laws and regulations. He was governed from inside by his relationship with his Father. He showed no fear of contamination from either an 'unclean' woman (Matthew 9:21) or a dead child (Matthew 9:25). During his lifetime, he clearly thought and talked about his impending death by crucifixion, but this was not a repetitive or intrusive thought of obsessive disorder, because he did not try to neutralize it, but accepted it, planned for it and taught his disciples about it.

In short, Jesus showed neither obsessive-compulsive disorder nor obsessional personality. We have tried, but can think of no other mental illness from which a reasonable person could claim that Jesus suffered. We therefore conclude that he experienced no mental illness.

Personality abnormality or disorder?

An article in *The Times* claimed that both candidates in the 2016 US presidential election were psychopaths.[9] What is significant for us is that the author also included Jesus in his list of 'psychopaths'. The method for carrying out this research was seriously flawed, but that is irrelevant for our purposes: what we note is that such a claim for Jesus could even have been made.

In this section we move away from examining mental illness to looking at personality disorder in relation to Jesus. To do this, we must build a working model for personality disorder: what is personality? What is abnormal personality? What traits of personality are significant in mental illness? What constitutes disorder of personality?

In describing personality, we will concentrate on only two aspects of personality: subjectively, it is 'the unique quality of the individual, his feelings and personal goals';[10] objectively, it is that person's persistent attitudes and behaviour as observed by others.

When we talk about normal personality, we should use the term 'normal' in its scientific sense, that is, the statistical norm. For example, an Englishman whose height is 5 ft 10 in. is normal; to be 6 ft 4 in. or 5 ft 4 in. is equally 'abnormal'. Stating that such people are 'abnormal' is not a value judgment, nor does it comment on whether they are taller or shorter than normal. Normality and abnormality of personality should be assessed in the same way.

Substantially more or less than normal of a personality characteristic is equally abnormal. Take, for example, as a fanciful measure of a personality characteristic, 'the milk of human kindness'. St Francis of Assisi had gallons of it – much *more* than a 'normal' person; Hitler had virtually none –

much *less* than normal. On this characteristic, they were both abnormal, but in different directions. If we look at personality this way, Jesus did not have a normal personality. His life and actions were far above the norm in quality.

From what we read of his personality, Jesus was sensitive to the needs of others, for example, the apostles, and able to feel their inner world.[11] He could be alone without feeling lonely. He was mature in his attachments – to the apostles, to women, to all those for whom he cared. He showed a combination of security and self-reliance, with an unbounded capacity for love and care for others. From his excellent childhood relationship with his mother he had a secure basis from which he could go out into the world, as is seen, for example, in his discussion with the teachers in the temple courts at the age of twelve (Luke 2:42–47).

Was Jesus abnormal in personality? The answer crucially depends on how you define both 'personality' and 'abnormal', but, in the statistical sense, he was a long way from the mean in personality, like his follower, St Francis of Assisi. The more important question, however, for our investigation into personality disorder, is: in what way did he deviate from the norm? What was his personality like? Did his personality result in distress to others or to himself?

The characteristic traits of Jesus' personality

Only some of the many personality traits described have implications for mental illness. We have already portrayed a possible trait: 'the milk of human kindness', and shown that through Jesus' unbounded capacity for love for others he was therefore, statistically, abnormal. However, this is of no psychiatric significance – as psychiatrists, we do not see people coming to consult us because they are too loving and charitable!

Only certain personality traits are recognized as having clinical significance. These were listed by Kurt Schneider in the mid-twentieth century,[12] and have formed the basis for the two official classifications of mental illness: the International Classification of Mental and Behavioral Disorders (ICD 10),[13] and the US Diagnostic and Statistical Manual of Mental Disorders (*DSM-5*).[14]

We know a lot about what Jesus was like: he taught with authority; he was clear and decisive – not in the slightest bit indecisive or vacillating (Matthew 7:29). His authority was undisputed, and what he said happened. For example, when he healed the centurion's servant, the employee of someone who is used to wielding power and showing complete trust, healing was immediate and total (Luke 7:1–10). Jesus' authority was acknowledged by his disciples: 'Master, Master, we're going to drown!' (Luke 8:24). In contemporary speech, Jesus would be described as having 'a commanding personality', which is what convinced the disciples to leave their work – fishing – and follow him to become 'fishers for people' (Luke 5:1–11). He was in command of every situation, for example, when he healed the paralysed man, saying, 'Your sins are forgiven' (Luke 5:23).

Although Jesus spoke and acted with authority, he was also supremely humble and did not impose his will. In his teaching about 'anyone who wants to be first', he hugged a child and recommended that his hearers welcome a child in his name, using children as a model for humility (Mark 9:35–37).

Although he was in control of every situation, Jesus was never a tyrant or dictator, but put himself in the position of a servant, even to the extent of giving his own life: he came 'to serve, and to give his life as a ransom for many' (Matthew 20:28). 'Whoever wants to be first must be your slave' (Matthew 20:27) was his message for those who want to take precedence.

The integrity of Jesus' character was recognized by his crafty enemies, who asked whether taxes should be paid to Caesar: 'Teacher, we know that you are a man of integrity. You aren't swayed by others, because you pay no attention to who they are; but you teach the way of God in accordance with the truth' (Mark 12:14). Jesus' response is a rhetorical tour de force (Mark 12:17).

There was a gentler side to Jesus' nature. When he wept over the fate of Jerusalem, this was not a sign of weakness (Luke 19:41). He had warned repeatedly of God's impending judgment; he had implored them to repent, but Jerusalem and the temple, the leaders of the nation, had resisted God's call. In the temple he finds only commerce, but no repentance. He cries for the innocent victims of the destruction of the city, 'Unless you repent, you too will all perish' (Luke 13:3, 5). When Jesus wept, he was identifying with the sorrow of others, for example, Martha and Mary after Lazarus had died (John 11:35), as we saw earlier.

Jesus was authentic in personality: genuine, consistent, true all through (see chapter 5). If there were a personality scale for authenticity, he would be at least two standard deviations above the norm: 'abnormal'. He was truthful, consistent, charitable and loyal in the extreme. From all these brief sketches of his personality, there are no hints that he might have suffered from the consequences of his personality, or caused others to suffer. For Jesus, there is no description of those abnormal personality characteristics that might cause psychological problems.

Personality disorder and its types

In order to build up a picture of what personality disorder is, we have looked at personality, abnormal personality and some of the traits that may be expressed in abnormal personality. Personality abnormality is part of that person's constitution. For abnormality to be recognized as personality disorder depends to a considerable extent on social circumstances: a person with highly abnormal personality characteristics in politics might be considered a criminal psychopath in another situation.

Personality disorder is present when the abnormality of personality causes the person himself or herself to suffer, or other people to suffer. There is an enduring pattern of seeing the world and acting that deviates markedly from the rest of that individual's social milieu and leads to significant distress or impairment in work, family or social functioning.

Jesus and personality disorder

Jesus was controversial and outspoken, and he demanded allegiance. He said, 'Do not suppose that I have come to bring peace to the earth. I did not come to bring peace, but a sword' (Matthew 10:34). His teaching was disturbing, then and now, and not comfortable or tranquil, but he was never irrational or inconsistent. The turbulence of his words arose from his message and not from abnormality of personality. His personality characteristics did not cause him or others to suffer. His suffering resulted from his determination to do his 'Father's will' – to fulfil his destiny.

To make a serious claim that Jesus suffered from personality disorder, one must specify what is meant by personality disorder, and what type of disorder it is. Of the two widely used classifications of mental disorders, we will look, very briefly, at *DSM-5*.[15] This lists ten separate types of personality disorder, organized within three clusters. We don't need to be concerned further with Cluster A, the 'odd, eccentric cluster', or Cluster C, the 'anxious, fearful cluster'. Jesus was not odd or eccentric, not remote or socially withdrawn from other people; there are many accounts of Jesus at meals, banquets and other social gatherings (Luke 14:1), and parables involving feasting (Luke 14:16–23). Celebrating and socializing were very much a part of Jesus' currency. The insights into individuals that Jesus showed were always practical, demonstrating that he understood people and their needs and motivations – the opposite end of the spectrum from Asperger's syndrome;[16] he formed excellent relationships with those whom he encountered. Neither did he show anxious or fearful traits – the very opposite, in fact, as he was courageous and confident, and yet had, and conveyed, a deep sense of peace, as we noted earlier.

Cluster B is the 'dramatic, emotional and erratic cluster'. Disorders in this cluster share problems with impulse control and emotional regulation; there may be dangerous outbursts of aggression or extravagant swings of mood. Arnold, aged thirty, had had many jobs, including a short stint as a social worker. Although very charming on first meeting, he regularly got into arguments with his boss and others in authority. He took money from the firm's charitable fund, and on one occasion, when he was very angry, he entered his work premises at night and vandalized the office. He could never sustain a lasting relationship with men or women. Throughout his life he blamed other people when anything went wrong. For example, when caught stealing, he blamed the company's poor accounting system. Arnold was unable to feel inside himself how others felt about the way he had treated them.

Can Jesus fit this category? Jesus himself taught his followers about genuineness and not play-acting when they were 'practising piety'. This is true for both giving money and praying to God – both should be done in private: 'Then your Father, who sees what is done in secret, will reward you'

(Matthew 6:4). He was always consistent, reliable and sensitive to the feelings of the other person.

Jesus was never impulsive in actions or in words. He told his disciples parables, the gist of which was that God is working but we must be patient (Matthew 13:24–33). Jesus has been accused of being petty and petulant in two stories that appear next to each other in Mark's Gospel (Mark 11:12–25). In the first, Jesus curses a fig tree for not bearing fruit, even though it was not the season for fruiting. In the second, he cleanses the temple of commerce. Both of these are factual accounts, which are also parables, and shed light on the coming of the kingdom. They both refer to the temple and the people of Israel, who were sometimes represented by a fig tree bearing fruit. Israel had become unfruitful and concerned with everyday human affairs rather than with God. In both episodes, Jesus was teaching, harking back to the Old Testament prophets and pointing forward to the coming kingdom.

He was prepared to be involved in conflict and stand on his own. He did not give in or weaken, but sustained his position with argument (Luke 11:42–54). None of the accounts suggests that Jesus was 'dramatic, emotional or erratic' in personality. He carried out actions and engaged in argument to achieve his aim, and he was equable in temperament. He neither sought nor avoided conflict. Throughout his ministry Jesus demonstrated sensitivity towards the weakness and distress of those around him. In this he showed exactly the opposite characteristics to those of psychopathy or personality disorder.

Not 'normal' personality, nor personality disordered, but the 'healthiest mind of all'

A child academically in the middle of the class may be described as being of 'normal intelligence'. In that sense, the brighter children are not normal, statistically, in intelligence. Jesus' personality was in part constitutional and in part developed through childhood and early adult life. It was perfectly suited for his active life of teaching and healing, leading his disciples and disputing with the authorities who had set themselves up in enmity towards him. In those personality traits that suggest mental illness he showed no abnormality, but in those characteristics that tend towards a loving relationship with people around him, he was superlative, well above normal. Personality does not affect what one believes, but it does affect how one believes it.

In chapter 2 we found no grounds for claiming that Jesus was mad or psychotic. In chapter 3 we have looked at other 'mental illnesses' and also at 'personality disorders', exploring what both terms mean. Again, we find that they were not present at any time in Jesus' story. To rephrase Pontius Pilate, we find no evidence of mental illness in him. Jesus, a revolutionary? Yes. A madman? No.

The theme of this book is that Jesus had not just a 'healthy mind', but the healthiest of all, and we describe that in the subsequent chapters. He was not just normal in mental health, but significantly above normal: the 'healthiest mind of all' – the Son of God, mature, stable and well adjusted.

4. THE TEST OF HIS CHARACTER: 'THE CROWDS WERE AMAZED . . . '

Einstein, who never professed to be a Christian, admitted to being 'enthralled by the luminous figure of the Nazarene'.[1] Similarly, Dostoyevsky wrote, 'I believe that there is nothing lovelier, deeper, more sympathetic, more rational, more manly, and more perfect than Christ. I say to myself with jealous love that not only is there no one else like Him, but that there could be no one.'[2]

What is it that makes Jesus so attractive and unique? Our purpose in this chapter is to explain how Jesus' character was so stable, mentally healthy and morally righteous that time and again it raised wonder and astonishment in the people who met him, a wonder that continued well after his death, as Einstein and Dostoyevsky witness.

We concluded the last chapter by affirming that Jesus was significantly above normal, with the 'healthiest mind of all'. But what is a healthy mind? The human personality, as we just saw, can be approached from different angles. In fact, assessment tools (psychological tests, clinical scales) give only partial information, not a full evaluation. This is why we need to define the main features of a well-adjusted, mature person.

We will summarize these indicators of maturity in five traits. In choosing them, we have tried to be eclectic and practical by focusing on those which are considered essential in most working models. Notice how they are in sharp contrast with their opposites, which express immaturity or a lack of adjustment:

1. humility: a right self-concept – no inflated ego
2. gentleness: a good capacity for self-control – no impulsiveness
3. love: a generous self-giving – no self-centredness
4. responsibility: a strong sense of commitment – no double-mindedness
5. patience: good tolerance of frustration – no wavering, no unsteadiness.

We believe that these five features find their maximum expression in Jesus. They are like a ladder where one step leads to the next one until it reaches the top, in this case the emotional balance and moral beauty of his personality. As a whole, they are an unparalleled demonstration of what being human is like.

1. Humility: the strength of a right self-concept

The only time Jesus referred to himself as a model to his disciples was when mentioning his humility and his gentleness: 'Learn from me, for I am gentle and humble in heart' (Matthew 11:29). This was the summary he made of his character. It was not by chance. These two traits are like the 'foundational couple' of our personality, because they have to do with our identity. Who am I? The answer to this question, the way I see myself, will greatly determine how I behave, react, feel and treat others. Self-concept sets the foundation of our emotional and moral make-up. Many disorders spring from disturbances at this basic level.

When Jesus states, 'I am humble', he is pointing to the core of his character. Being humble is exactly the opposite of an inflated ego, which is the defining feature of a paranoid personality. Humility is the cardinal expression of a right self-concept, and it becomes the necessary starting point for growth into maturity.

An appropriate self-perception is a sort of fertile ground where all the other healthy seeds of the character may grow. True humility leads to meekness, and then it nourishes a spirit of love that eventually brings forth patience and endurance and a life of service to others. This is why Jesus was so emphatic when he told his disciples, 'Learn humility and gentleness from my example.' Eventually Jesus gave them an amazing lesson on practical humility when he washed their feet (a story we will consider further at the end of this book).

Also, in his public ministry, Jesus commended humility as the pre-eminent characteristic of God's kingdom. Remember that he invested in children such value that it was said, 'Only he among the world's religious and ethical teachers has set a little child before us as our model.'[3]

Humility, coupled with gentleness, is probably one of the most attractive features in a person's character. You feel immediately at ease with someone who is sincerely humble and gentle. Because Jesus was humble, he could relate meaningfully with prostitutes and 'professors' (Nicodemus), rich and poor, children and adults, Jews and Samaritans. There is something mysteriously attractive in the humble person.

But, you may say, isn't humility a weakness? In a world that worships all kinds of self-assertion, we need to remember that being humble is an expression of strength. It is much more difficult to be humble than to be arrogant and harbour feelings of superiority. Humility does not come automatically; pride and arrogance do. Nevertheless, many are unable to understand – or to accept – that being humble is the foundation of moral authority and true strength. Illustrious atheists, like Nietzsche, who defined the good as the 'will to power', ridicule Christ precisely for his apparent weakness.[4]

From his birth in a stable until his death on a cross, the whole life of Jesus was a most powerful lesson in humility. The apostle Paul expressed it in memorable words:

> [Jesus] who, being in very nature God,
> > did not consider equality with God something
> > > to be used to his own advantage;
> > rather, he made himself nothing
> > > by taking the very nature of a servant . . .
> > > he humbled himself.
> (Philippians 2:6–8)

This humility nourished Jesus' servanthood. The spirit of a servant was a hallmark of Jesus' life and work, rejecting always all forms of human power or dominion. He explicitly said, 'The Son of Man did not come to be served, but to serve' (Matthew 20:28). Such servanthood sprang from his being humble and gentle in heart.[5]

So the humility that comes from an accurate assessment of oneself is the first evidence of maturity. Its opposite, an inflated ego, is the seed of a paranoid personality and is found in many emotional disturbances.

2. Gentleness: the strength of self-control

Humility and gentleness make a couple; they go together, as in Paul's words: 'By the meekness and gentleness of Christ, I appeal to you . . .' (2 Corinthians 10:1). If humility has to do with self-perception, then meekness has to do with self-control. Being humble is an inner attitude; meekness is the outward expression of such an attitude. Being gentle, considerate and courteous to others is the natural outcome of being humble. It is a logical sequence: when you have learnt to assess yourself correctly, then you are able to treat others properly too.

The word 'gentle' means having a kind or tender temperament. Jesus was indeed a model of gentleness in all his relationships, including with his enemies. Meekness is not a weakness either. Only strong characters are able to display the wide range of moral qualities that meekness embraces.

How was gentleness expressed in Jesus' life? Like a rainbow showing the beauty of its varied colours, Jesus' meekness radiates self-control, peace, rest and tenderness (sensitivity). Through these four traits we will discover how Jesus, the healthiest mind of all, mastered areas where we are struggling time and again.

Self-control
Self-control is the opposite of impulsiveness, and it is one of the best tests by which to measure the strength of a character. A mature person has learnt to 'be quick to listen, slow to speak and slow to become angry' (James 1:19). On the other hand, the immature character shows choleric reactions and is given to childish tantrums, especially when things do not happen as they would like.

If anyone has ever proved to be a self-controlled person, no doubt this has to be Jesus. He was such an example of self-control, even when slandered and tortured, that he was compared to a lamb, 'the Lamb of God'. Notice what the apostle Peter writes of him: 'When they hurled their insults at him, he did not retaliate; when he suffered, he made no threats. Instead, he entrusted himself to him who judges justly' (1 Peter 2:23).

Jesus got angry at times, but he never lost control of his reactions. Even when he drove the money changers out of the temple, we do not see signs or symptoms of an intermittent explosive disorder.[6] Notice that Jesus did a careful inspection the day before: 'Jesus . . . went into the temple courts. He looked around at everything, but since it was already late, he went out to Bethany with the Twelve' (Mark 11:11). So his behaviour was not a sudden choleric reaction; Jesus had long hours to meditate on what he had seen in the temple the previous evening. Then, the following day, 'he made a whip out of cords, and drove all from the temple courts', saying, 'Stop turning my Father's house into a market!' (John 2:15–16). He was certainly very angry and acted accordingly, but it was not blind rage, he never lost control of his words or actions and he even articulated a reasonable argument: 'You are making my house a den of robbers' (Matthew 21:13), quoting the prophet Jeremiah (Jeremiah 7:11). The only harm he caused was to the economic interests of the money changers.

Jesus' meekness was not something passive, a matter of 'stop doing', avoiding the wrong word or reaction. It also meant sharing two great treasures of a healthy mind that he had in abundance: peace and rest. In fact, on several occasions Jesus invites his followers to enjoy his peace and to rest in him.

Peace

Meekness radiates peace. Nowhere in the Gospels does Jesus seem restless, fearful or nervous. He had peace inside, and he shared it. He radiated peace wherever he went, because his words and deeds brought forth healing and restoration, hope and life.

Jesus remained serene and calm in the midst of the most adverse circumstances: heavy storms that put his life at risk, fierce hostility from the religious leaders who tried to kill him several times, an ignominious trial that led to his death. Only once do we see Jesus deeply troubled and anxious for himself, and that was just before his death.

Rest

The meekness of Jesus was likewise a source of rest: 'Come to me, all you who are weary and burdened, and I will give you rest. Take my yoke upon you and learn from me, for I am gentle and humble in heart, and you will find rest for your souls' (Matthew 11:28–29).

Notice the close relationship between his being 'gentle and humble' and the rest that springs from it. He was able to invite his disciples to rest because his character was in itself a source of stillness. Also, his own behaviour was a model to them: 'Then, because so many people were coming and going that they did not even have a chance to eat, he said to them, "Come with me by yourselves to a quiet place and get some rest"' (Mark 6:31).

Jesus lived a very active life, but not a stressful life. Actually, he never seemed to be in a hurry. We discover in him a balance between intense work and rest. With the exception mentioned in chapter 2 (the event recorded in Mark 3:20–21), he never neglected the physical, spiritual and emotional renewal that came from rest and prayer. The secret of such a healthy balance lies in the fact that he was well aware of the difference between *chronos*, 'clock-driven time', and *kairos*, 'the right hour, the suitable moment'. Jesus does not appear to us as 'a driven personality', permanently on the edge of burnout, but rather as a diligent steward, ready to make the best of every suitable opportunity. This mastery of time is indeed evidence of a stable mind.

Sensitivity and tenderness

Jesus' meekness also radiated sensitivity. The word used by Paul to refer to the 'gentleness of Christ' (2 Corinthians 10:1) can also be rendered as tenderness, goodness, kindness. The idea is that of a person with a tender heart whose empathy and sympathy are easily aroused. Its opposite is a tough, rude character who cares very little about others.

The serenity of Jesus did not lead him to a lack of sensitivity or to impassivity. Jesus' peace was not a stoic or nirvana type of attitude. He carefully appreciated the beauty in nature (flowers, birds, clouds); he rejoiced at a wedding banquet; he was aware when his disciples needed food or rest; he cared about his mother when he was dying on the cross, and about children.

Likewise, the parables he shared reveal a tender heart (the great joy of finding a lost sheep or a lost coin, the moving return of the prodigal son and the delicate care of the good shepherd).

Jesus also showed great sensitivity in situations of evil, injustice, sickness, calamity or death. One striking example was his reaction when his friend Lazarus died: 'When Jesus saw her weeping, and the Jews who had come along with her also weeping, he was deeply moved in spirit and troubled . . . Jesus, once more deeply moved, came to the tomb' (John 11:33, 38). The word for 'deeply moved' conveys the idea of a very intense disturbance. He also wept over the tragic future he foresaw for the city of Jerusalem.

In short, his heart and mind were always very perceptive of the good and the evil around him, and such awareness led Jesus to mourn with those who mourned and to rejoice with those who rejoiced. His sharp perception of reality drove him to compassion as well as to action.

3. Love: the strength of self-giving

The maturity and the moral beauty of Jesus' character reach their climax with love: 'A new command I give you: love one another. As I have loved you, so you must love one another. By this everyone will know that you are my disciples, if you love one another' (John 13:34–35). A right self-concept – humility – and a good capacity for self-control – gentleness – lead to a generous self-giving, our third step in the ladder. Love is the pre-eminent, distinguishing characteristic of the life and teaching of Jesus. Love reveals the summit of his exceptional character. Everything in him revolves around love because he gave precedence to love. Love is the motivation and the culmination of all that he was – all that he taught and did. Jesus summarized the whole duty of humankind as loving God and one's neighbour (Matthew 22:37–40). No wonder that Christianity is recognized historically as the religion of love. Love is supposed to be the distinguishing feature of everyone related to Jesus.

Love and maturity: Jesus, the opposite of Narcissus

Love is the paramount expression of psychological (and spiritual) maturity. It is a basic evidence of adulthood in the same measure that self-centredness is a key evidence of childishness or immaturity. The renowned psychiatrist

Armand Nicholi writes, 'Self-giving love is essential in all mature human relationships.'[7]

The capacity to love others is the opposite of narcissistic self-love. The story of Narcissus, an ancient Greek myth, contains a striking lesson on the nature and frequent outcome of self-love. Narcissus was a handsome but proud young man who disdained those who loved him. Once he saw his own reflection in a pool of water and fell in love with it, not realizing it was merely an image. Unable to leave the beauty of his reflection, he stared at it until he died. He was unable to love others because he was too much in love with himself. This is usually the outcome of narcissism: a useless life, wasted in the slavery of self-centredness and self-love. The contrast between Jesus and Narcissus could not be sharper. They are poles apart in the expression and direction of love.

You may object here that the teaching of Jesus sounds narcissistic because it was very self-centred. And you are right. He was constantly talking about himself and he referred to his person as the special 'I am' several times. Is this a contradiction? How could this most humble and loving man be talking about himself so often? As we anticipated in the preface, this great paradox will give us the key that discloses his extraordinary character and will eventually allow us to understand his claims in chapter 9.

Corrie ten Boom: the love of Jesus in the Nazi concentration camps

The love Jesus taught and incarnated with his life is agape love:

> It is a disinterested, objective willing of the best for a person, regardless how one feels toward him or her. Unlike the other forms of love (affection, passion, friendship), agape does not

require previous positive feelings. It involves primarily one's will and one's actions.[8]

It is not an emotion, but a choice; it focuses not just on friends, but on everyone, including your enemies. Jesus summarized it in a memorable sentence known as the 'Golden Rule': 'In everything, do to others what you would have them do to you, for this sums up the Law and the Prophets' (Matthew 7:12). Agape love implies looking out and caring for your neighbour, even to the point of death: 'Greater love has no one than this: to lay down one's life for one's friends' (John 15:13).

Is this love an impossible ideal in our modern life? Not at all! The startling story of Corrie ten Boom is a challenging illustration in comparatively recent times of how Jesus' love is possible, and how it continues to transform individuals as well as groups. Together with her family, this Dutch lady risked her life to save many Jews from Nazi cruelty. First, she helped them to escape, providing ways to leave the city. When this was no longer possible, she hid them in the family's ramshackle house. In total over 700 passed through the house. A secret room – the hiding place[9] – was built behind her bedroom.

Betrayed by an informer, the ten Booms were arrested. Corrie was taken with her sister Betsie to Ravensbrück concentration camp. There 'they changed the atmosphere of their hut by showing love to the other prisoners and organizing daily gatherings from Scripture reading and prayer . . . Because the room was infested with fleas, the guards never came in to stop them.'[10] After the war, Corrie became involved in the care and rehabilitation of prisoners of war.

The story of this courageous woman and her family is an amazing example of the love Jesus preached and lived out.

Let us see now how Jesus himself described the practice of this love.

Jesus explains the practice of love: compassion in action

The cornerstone of this new love is a self-giving heart and a proactive attitude that takes the initiative: it requires work. Love must be expressed in positive attitudes and concrete actions, not just feelings or words. When Jesus was asked about love, he explained it with two vivid stories: the parables of the prodigal son and the good Samaritan. These two narratives are a superb mirror of Christ's character, reflecting his loving heart and confirming how mature the man Jesus was. They illuminate the practice of love in an unsurpassable way, and have become a universal reference in the understanding of what love is like.

> On one occasion an expert in the law . . . asked Jesus, 'And who is my neighbour?'
>
> In reply Jesus said: 'A man was going down from Jerusalem to Jericho, when he was attacked by robbers. They stripped him of his clothes, beat him and went away, leaving him half-dead. A priest happened to be going down the same road, and when he saw the man, he passed by on the other side. So too, a Levite, when he came to the place and saw him, passed by on the other side. But a Samaritan, as he travelled, came where the man was; and when he saw him, he took pity on him. He went to him and bandaged his wounds, pouring on oil and wine. Then he put the man on his own donkey, brought him to an inn and took care of him. The next day he took out two denarii and gave them to the innkeeper. "Look after him," he said, "and when I return, I will reimburse you for any extra expense you may have."

'Which of these three do you think was a neighbour to the man who fell into the hands of robbers?'

The expert in the law replied, 'The one who had mercy on him.'

Jesus told him, 'Go and do likewise.'

(Luke 10:25–37)

Notice also this meaningful paragraph in the parable of the prodigal son (Luke 15:11–32):

So [the son] got up and went to his father.

But while he was still a long way off, his father saw him and was filled with compassion for him; he ran to his son, threw his arms around him and kissed him . . . and said: 'For this son of mine was dead and is alive again; he was lost and is found.' So they began to celebrate.

The backbone of Jesus' love

The distinctive features of Jesus' love shine brightly in these two narratives. We will see them repeated throughout his life:

- **Mercy and compassion.** 'He was moved to mercy and compassion.' The word 'moved' tells us about his motivation. Mercy and compassion were the driving force that motivated Jesus' love. The expression 'he had compassion on them', repeated several times in the Gospels, conveys a great intensity of feeling, a deep affection springing from his innermost heart.
- **Grace.** Jesus was a man 'full of grace and truth' (John 1:14). This is how John summarized the character of his Master. In all his relationships, even in controversy and disagreement, Jesus reflected grace by treating everyone

with dignity. He did not put down love and pick up wrath when talking about morality or relating to sinners. Grace and mercy were so important for him that he urged his followers to be merciful too:

> Blessed are the merciful
>   for they will be shown mercy.
> (Matthew 5:7)

The grace of Jesus is 'Christianity's best gift to the world, a spiritual nova[11] in our midst exerting a force stronger than vengeance, stronger than racism, stronger than hate'.[12]

- **Forgiveness.** Grace makes a forgiving spirit possible. The parable of the prodigal son has touched the hearts of many people deeply because it conveys a very powerful message of forgiveness. Forgiveness illuminates everything in this narrative and turns the dark areas of the son's behaviour into a joyful feast. Forgiveness transforms wounds into scars. Forgiveness was so much at the core of Jesus' life that he died forgiving his enemies.
- **Unconditional, without discrimination.** Both the Samaritan and the father of the prodigal son show a kind of love that has no barriers or limits. Nothing hindered their works of love. In the same way, Jesus loved without any discrimination, as we will see in the next chapter. In Christ's estimation, our neighbour is everyone. He loved regardless of the outcome of this love.

The warmth, empathy and self-giving that highlighted Jesus' life are at the opposite pole from the aloofness, self-centredness and loose affective links that characterize personality disorders and psychosis. If it is true, and we believe that it is, that the more able you are to give and receive love, the healthier you can be considered, then Jesus is indeed the healthiest mind of all.

4. Responsibility: the strength of commitment

'Why were you searching for me? . . . Didn't you know I had to be in my Father's house?' (Luke 2:49). A striking sentence coming from a twelve-year-old boy! To our surprise, these are the first recorded words spoken by Jesus. The story of the boy in the temple is quite well known: the child had got lost during the pilgrimage to Jerusalem, and his parents searched for him anxiously. After three days they found him at the temple, 'sitting among the teachers, listening to them and asking them questions' (Luke 2:46). The reaction of the people around is noteworthy because we will see it again in his adult life: 'Everyone who heard him was amazed at his understanding and his answers' (2:47). And not only the people, but also 'his parents were astonished'. Incidentally, these comments provide evidence that Jesus had very high intelligence, a privileged mind able to discuss matters with adults in a way that was very unusual for a boy of this age.

A firm sense of responsibility is the fourth step in the ladder of maturity. In Jesus we see it manifested in three features that reveal a strength of commitment where there was no place for double-mindedness:

1. determination: commitment to his life purpose
2. obedience: commitment to his Father's will
3. faithfulness: commitment to his people.

Determination: commitment to his life purpose

It cannot be by chance that the incident of the young Jesus at the temple is the only story we have about his childhood. It is a highly significant event and contains a strong message: even from childhood, Jesus was conscious of his mission, and this gave him a clear sense of commitment. His life was purpose driven from the beginning, for he was fully aware of the unique task he was to accomplish: 'I have brought you glory on earth by finishing the work you gave me to do' (John 17:4). As we said earlier, never was anyone else so consistently goal-directed.

Notice this sense of responsibility in his reply: 'Didn't you know I had to be in my Father's house?' (Luke 2:49). It is amazing for a boy to show such a level of insight and maturity regarding his vocation.

Notice also the last sentence in the text: 'Then he went down to Nazareth with [his parents] and was obedient to them' (Luke 2:51). There are no signs of a defiant attitude, or opposition, but rather submission to his parents. As Joseph Ratzinger comments in his book on the infancy of Jesus, in this incident we do not see 'an act of rebellion to his parents, but an act of obedience to His Father'.[13] 'My food . . . is to do the will of him who sent me and to finish his work' (John 4:34).

Obedience: commitment to his Father's will

The deep awareness of his purpose gave Jesus a strong determination to obey 'the will of my Father' (see John 5:30; 6:38). The firm and resolute conduct of the younger Jesus in the temple continued in adult life, and he pursued God's will in order to fulfil it until the end.

This commitment implied a refusal of any compromise or short cut. As noted in chapter 1, there were several occasions when he was seriously tempted either to step back or to take easier roads that would spare him a lot of suffering. He said 'no' to these temptations with exemplary assertiveness. No weak or unstable person would have been able to respond to such emotional and spiritual harassment with the firmness that Jesus showed.

Let us remember, for example, when he was tempted to bypass the cross. The assault of Satan was very intelligent: he shrewdly tempted Jesus in two sensitive areas at this initial stage of his public life – his identity and his ministry (Matthew 4:1–11). Jesus refused to compromise: 'Immediately, instinctively, vehemently, he rejected each temptation. There was no need to discuss or to negotiate.'[14] His priorities were so clearly set in his mind that he was able to say 'yes', 'no' or 'not yet' without any hesitation. No signs of an insecure, wavering character whatsoever here.

Another example of the same determination occurred when the crowd wanted to make him king after the feeding of the 5,000 (John 6:1–15). He resolutely escaped the subtle temptation of human power that would distract him from the real purpose of his life. His determination to obey allowed him to be 'faithful to the one who appointed him' (Hebrews 3:2).

Faithfulness: commitment to his people

Commitment is also expressed in faithfulness to people. Jesus' closest disciples soon realized that he was a trustworthy person. Had he been emotionally unstable, he would never have aroused such confidence. Unstable people are easily influenced and double-minded. The apostles saw in Jesus a most reliable master and friend: 'Lord, to whom shall we go? You have the words of eternal life' (John 6:68).

So here we have a man with clear priorities since childhood and a firm resolution to accomplish them. He is neither thrown off course nor distracted by short cuts to success. He is single-minded and self-disciplined, spares no effort and makes sacrifices in order to serve 'the one who sent me', and he inspires in his disciples a thorough trust. Certainly, no-one with serious mental instability would display such an overwhelming example of responsibility and commitment.

5. Patience: the strength of perseverance and endurance

Patience is the opposite of a low tolerance to frustration. It is the ability to continue until the end once you start a task, regardless of the obstacles. In anything you do it is important to start well, but it is even more important to end well: 'May the Lord direct your hearts . . . into Christ's perseverance' (2 Thessalonians 3:5). Patience, the last step in our ladder, is a very reliable indicator of maturity because it tests both perseverance and endurance. It correlates very highly with self-control (meekness) and with determination (responsibility). In practice, they form a kind of cluster that lies behind the attractiveness of many mature men and women. Psychologists often refer to this cluster with the term 'ego strength'.

Likewise, there is a close relationship between patience and love. Remarkably, Paul writes that the first evidence of love is patience: 'Love is patient' (1 Corinthians 13:4). The connection between these virtues reaches its maximum splendour in Jesus' character. He was indeed a man of love and patience; his loving heart made him a most patient person.

Now what is patience? What kind of patience did Jesus show? To be patient encompasses two complementary attitudes that go together like the two sides of a coin.

Patience is perseverance

Patience implies, first of all, perseverance or steadfastness. It was the attitude that nourished Jesus' determination to 'pursue till the end'. Patience enabled him to accomplish the full purpose of his life (John 17:4).

An immature, unsteady person gives up as soon as the first difficulties arise. Jesus himself warned his followers about the vital importance of this kind of perseverance: 'Stand firm [be patient] and you will win life' (Luke 21:19). However, if we limit patience to this dimension, we miss the other side of the coin.

Patience is endurance

Perseverance must be accompanied by endurance. Jesus' patience was indeed much richer and deeper than mere perseverance. The original meaning of the word is 'greatness of spirit', and it is the term Paul uses when he says, 'Love is patient.' It refers to a strong spirit, remaining long-suffering and firm in adversity, a person who does not give up or waver when facing difficult circumstances. It is exactly the contrary of being 'feeble in spirit', a coward who 'drowns in a glass of water'.

Patience does not admit defeat, but fights. Rather than crumbling in the face of adversity, it gains strength and, instead of being passive, actively looks for solutions.

Patience brings forth courage

Jesus was a brave man. As we said earlier, it is a mistake to interpret his meekness as weakness. In Jesus' character, meekness and courage go hand in hand in a harmonious balance. He did not hesitate, for example, to refer to Herod as a fox (Luke 13:31–32).

We will consider the exceptional courage Jesus showed as he faced torture and martyrdom later. Just notice now how he approached his cruel death: 'he steadfastly set his face to go to Jerusalem' (Luke 9:51, KJV). We do not see the slightest sign of cowardice in him. Patience strengthened him until the end.

Apologist Os Guinness describes the followers of Christ as 'impossible people', those who have 'hearts that can melt with compassion, but with faces like flint and backbones of steel who are unmanipulable, unbribable, undeterrable and unclubbable, without ever losing the gentleness, the mercy, the grace and the compassion of our Lord'.[15] I cannot think of a better summary of the character of Jesus himself. No wonder people felt 'astonished' and 'amazed' in his presence. Certainly you would never have such a feeling of wonder with a mentally sick or immature person.

As an artist starts with a sketch, now we have the outline of the basic traits of Jesus' character. The whole picture will be developed as we continue to consider his life and work, his relationships, the way he faced adversity, his influence and his claims. Then we will see that Jesus was not only *fully* human, but *perfectly* human. The quality of his humanity was superior. As the theologian M. J. Erickson points out, 'Jesus is not only as human as we are; He is more human. Our humanity is not a standard by which we are to measure His. His humanity, true and unadulterated, is the standard by which we are to be measured.'[16] Only when the portrait is finished will we be able to contemplate these moral and emotional qualities fully displayed, because in Jesus, more than in anyone else, the proverb is fulfilled:

The path of the righteous is like the morning sun,
    shining ever brighter till the full light of day.
(Proverbs 4:18)

5. THE TEST OF A CONSISTENT LIFE: 'WHAT EVIL HAS HE DONE? I HAVE FOUND NO CRIME IN HIM'

As former US President Abraham Lincoln once said, 'You can fool all the people some of the time and some of the people all the time, but you cannot fool all the people all the time.'[1] The overall view of someone's life is indeed that person's best moral and emotional portrait. You catch a reliable glimpse of moral uprightness and emotional stability through words and acts.

A healthy mind should be shown through a consistent life. Psychological balance – and moral goodness – need to be proved by the behaviour and trajectory of a life. Besides character, way of being, a person's mental stability is revealed by words and deeds. The way you are, how you speak and how you behave provide us with a very helpful 'tripod' to assess a person's emotional health.

Our main question in this chapter, therefore, must be: what do the deeds and the 'discourse' of Jesus tell us about him? Are there any indicators of contradictory or inconsistent behaviour? Do we find a dichotomy or split between his personality and his life?

Two testimonies, coming from opposite poles, bear witness to the moral quality and consistency of Jesus' life. On the one hand, Pontius Pilate, the Roman governor of Judea, made this statement while judging Jesus: 'What evil has he done? I have found in him no crime' (Luke 23:22, RSV). Strikingly, he declared Jesus innocent on several occasions. On the other hand, the apostle Peter, who had been at Jesus' side for three years, summed up his life thus: 'God anointed Jesus of Nazareth with the Holy Spirit and power, and . . . he went around doing good and healing all who were under the power of the devil, because God was with him' (Acts 10:38).

We can say of Jesus with total conviction what someone said about the Jewish-Christian philosopher Emmanuel Levinas: 'His life was his best book.' What can we read in Jesus' 'book'? What is the evidence for such an exceptionally righteous life?

Let us look at some basic indicators of health in Jesus' life. To begin with, we must highlight three general traits that enfold his entire life like a framework:

1. **Purpose:** a life with meaning. Jesus was not an existential tramp or a wanderer.
2. **Fullness:** a full and fruitful life. Jesus didn't fritter away his time.
3. **Balance:** a centred life. Jesus was not an eccentric.

A life with a purpose

Jesus' life had very clear objectives from the beginning, even from his childhood, as we saw earlier. A distinct sense of purpose and direction led him to act at all times within a carefully prepared framework. There was a well-defined trajectory. We do not see a Jesus without aim, like an existential wanderer who doesn't know what to do with his life. Regrettably, this is the condition of many individuals with psychosis who wander through life with a misguided purpose.

This framework is well described in what John Stott calls 'The Nazareth Manifesto'.[2] This text contains a remarkable summary of the ministry that Jesus would develop. It is like the index entry of the book of his life where we find a precise description of his 'agenda':

And the scroll of the prophet Isaiah was handed to him. Unrolling it, he found the place where it is written:

'The Spirit of the Lord is on me,
    because he has anointed me
    to proclaim good news to the poor.
He has sent me to proclaim freedom for the prisoners
    and recovery of sight for the blind,
to set the oppressed free,
    to proclaim the year of the Lord's favour.'
(Luke 4:17–19)

This passage is mentioned by three of the Gospel writers. Matthew and Mark include it in the closing part of their Gospels, while Luke places it at the beginning of Jesus' ministry. These locations affirm the idea of a framework that encompasses his life trajectory, akin to a programme to accomplish. A clear vision, and strict obedience to this proposition, formed the main theme of his life's book.

The Nazareth Manifesto describes clearly the 'what for' of Jesus' life, but it also gives us the clue to his motivation, the 'why'. Jesus never claimed that the primary purpose of his teaching or healing was to make this world a better place in which to live. His motivation was not merely social. There was a deeper reason for his doing good to everyone. His desire to serve others sprang from his wish to serve and obey his Father. He had come to fulfil the prophecy of Isaiah. His 'doing good and healing all' was part of being the willing servant. His profound humanity was a result of his profound spirituality.

A full and fruitful life

Apart from purpose, Jesus' life had content. It was a full and fruitful life, abounding in all kinds of good works, a life with a great impact among his contemporaries. Indeed, both aspects go hand in hand. This clarity of purpose results in an abundant content. People with chronic psychosis usually lead erratic lives, and reap a poor harvest. Sometimes stars shine in their life, or they may have occasional bursts of creativity or activity, but this is the exception in the book of their life. Jesus' life, on the other hand, is a shining light in which no darkness can be found.

There was no place for apathy or idleness in his daily routine. A good use of time and opportunities was his chief concern. Jesus knew nothing of the lack of enthusiasm and energy of those who are depressed, incapable of fulfilling their good desires, even the smallest ones. He also knew nothing of the social isolation of someone with psychosis, incapable of relating to other people. We do not see in him any acts lacking in significance, or attention-seeking histrionic gestures. Everything he did conformed to a double purpose: to serve and give life. Jesus lived to serve others because he 'did not come to be served, but to serve, and to give his life as a ransom for many' (Mark 10:45). Jesus fully accomplished the agenda of his life.

A balanced life

One of the most frequent traits in people suffering from psychosis or serious personality disorder is their tendency to have eccentric or marginalized lifestyles. In contrast, balance is the capacity to avoid such extremes. The word that best reflects this idea in the Gospels is 'wise'. Being wise is an approach to life that expresses balance, stability and trustworthiness.

Jesus loved balance. We can see this from various situations where he referred to this attitude of being wise. He associated it with virtues such as faithfulness (Matthew 25:1–12), in contrast with weaknesses like being foolish. This idea is well developed, for example, in the account of the two foundations: 'A wise man built his house on the rock . . . yet it did not fall, because it had its foundation on the rock . . . a foolish man built his house on sand . . . that house . . . fell with a great crash' (Matthew 7:24–27). According to the text, the opposite of being wise is to be foolish, the typical attitude of an irresponsible person.

Jesus' life demonstrates a constant balance between opposite poles, an amazing blend of authority and humility, depth and simplicity, firmness and tolerance, mercy and justice, meekness and courage, passion and serenity, tradition breaking and submission.

Jesus was a radical but not an extremist. He was indeed a master in resolving the tension between extremes, a model of equanimity, although this did not prevent him from being, at times, a radical. So Jesus was well balanced and radical at the same time. As Joseph Ratzinger expressed it, 'In Jesus we see the conjunction between radical innovation and equally radical constancy.'[3] How can this be? The word 'radical' comes from the Latin term for 'root'. Jesus was a radical because he always went deep into the root of every person or situation. His penetrating gaze and discernment allowed him to reach the roots without losing his sense of balance. Jesus always went to the bottom, never to the sides (extremes), a radical, but not an extremist. This is one of the most striking characteristics of his life and a remarkable sign of his mental health. Only a person with a marked internal equilibrium could display such a balanced life.

The life of a mentally ill person, especially someone suffering from psychosis or personality disorder, is a long way from possessing these three characteristics. On the contrary, we often witness feelings of frustration and the sense of a wasted life. What a contrast with the words of Jesus before he died: 'I have brought you glory on earth by finishing the work you gave me to do' (John 17:4). In fact, it was precisely in his last few days – and hours – that Jesus uttered some of the most profound and memorable discourses.

We don't see the slightest evidence of any mental deterioration in Jesus' story. In him we find full consistency between being and behaving, words and works, throughout his life.

So purpose, fullness and balance constitute what we may call the general characteristics of health in Jesus' life. Now we are going to consider some more specific traits by examining the diverse aspects of his public life.

The three great areas of the human mind – intellect, emotions and will – are affected to varying degrees in mental illnesses. Disorganized or incoherent thinking, difficulty in feeling or expressing emotions (affective flattening), as well as a decrease in will-power (apathy), are key symptoms of various mental illnesses, as considered earlier in chapters 1–3. In contrast, the following are indicators of mental health:

- a pattern of lucid and coherent thinking;
- a strong desire to help and do good to others;
- a rich capacity for feeling and expressing affection.

These three aspects feature significantly in each of the main areas of Jesus' ministry: as teacher, as healer and as restorer of marginalized lives.

1. The admired teacher: a lucid mind

Teaching and preaching were two of the core activities in Jesus' life. It is through his words and sayings that we have a clear manifestation of his brilliant mind and moral integrity. Jesus always displayed thinking that was lucid in its content, persuasive in its form and powerful in its results: '[The people] were astonished at his teaching, for his word was with authority' (Luke 4:32, RSV). We never see the bizarre, illogical or chaotic thinking of psychosis, the arrogance and inflated ego of paranoid personality, the egotism and coldness of psychopathy, or the vacillation and inconclusiveness of neurosis.

The coherence of his discourse, the ethical richness of his teachings and the profound influence of his words have no comparison or parallel in any other teacher in history. Moreover, highly respected non-Christian characters like Gandhi recognized that they had found in the teachings of Christ the main source of their ethical inspiration. The figure of Christ as teacher assumes a universal dimension that transcends time, religions and cultures.

Great impact
The reactions of admiration to Jesus the teacher and preacher were many. His language, simple but profound, humble but

with authority, capable of expressing great truths in simple stories, reached everyone. For example, at the end of the Sermon on the Mount we read, 'When Jesus had finished saying these things, the crowds were amazed at his teaching, because he taught as one who had authority, and not as their teachers of the law' (Matthew 7:28–29). On another occasion the temple guards were so amazed by his words that they refrained from carrying out the orders of the Pharisees to detain him and offered this explanation instead: 'No one ever spoke the way this man does' (John 7:46).

It wasn't just a question of admiration, but also of impact and influence. Nicodemus, for instance, a religious scholar and distinguished teacher, said to Jesus, 'Rabbi, we know that you are a teacher who has come from God' (John 3:2). Even his opponents acknowledged the power and influence of his teaching: '"Teacher," they said, "we know that you are a man of integrity and that you teach the way of God in accordance with the truth"' (Matthew 22:16).

Great wisdom

There are many aspects that we could highlight of Jesus as teacher. The scope of this book, however, requires us to adhere to those traits connected with his mental lucidity and moral goodness. Three methods in his teaching draw our attention as psychiatrists because they are only accessible to people with great wisdom and mental stability:

1. the wise use of parables;
2. the sharp reasoning in controversies;
3. the closeness of the mentor to his apostles.

He used the above three ad hoc, depending on the listeners he had before him. Jesus knew how to adapt equally to the simple understanding of the crowds, to the bad intentions of his opponents, or to the specific needs of his apostles. This triple formula provides a brilliant portrait of the excellence and balance Jesus displayed as teacher and preacher.

The wise use of parables. Jesus' capacity to communicate shines brilliantly in the use of parables: 'With many similar parables Jesus spoke the word to them, as much as they could understand. He did not say anything to them without using a parable' (Mark 4:33–34). Experts in literary criticism tell us that a good use of figures of speech is an art that distinguishes a good writer or communicator.

Jesus' skill in teaching through parables demonstrates not only the lucidity of his thinking, but also his emotional intelligence. His teaching in parables is splendid, becoming a sort of banquet to the reader of the Gospels, although not only a literary banquet, but also an ethical and spiritual one. The parables of Jesus contain an unparalleled corpus of teaching which is essential for human beings in order to relate with God and with their neighbour.

The sharp reasoning in controversies. In his controversies with the scribes and Pharisees, Jesus displayed an extraordinarily clever use of reasoning. Such rapidity in argument is only possible in a mind with a robust capacity for reasoning. Such a mind is certainly unimaginable in someone with mental deterioration. In controversy, the reaction times are very short and require quick mental reflexes. Jesus was a great controversialist.[4] His enemies never managed to defeat him with the power of words, only with the power of violence (the cross).

Debating, arguing and answering questions were an important part of Jesus' teaching. He not only faced controversy with total naturalness, but also took it to be an integral part of his discourse. Some of his deepest insights came as a result of these controversies. He never avoided being confronted by people who were interested not in discussing things, but only in accusing him. Jesus had the courage, the willingness and the capacity to face controversy successfully. Here we have another indicator of emotional stability: a typical characteristic of immature or unstable people is their lack of capacity to confront criticism and tolerate different points of view from their own.

In our opinion, Jesus' discussions and controversies with the religious leaders constitute another solid piece of evidence of his mental stability: here we contemplate not only the lucidity of a powerful thinker, but also the self-control of a mature character.

The closeness of the mentor to his apostles. Jesus did not limit his teaching to public speaking or to endless controversies, but devoted a good deal of his ministry to modelling to a few chosen people, the apostles. Jesus was a great mentor. He well knew the importance of learning from role models. If Christianity is essentially being like Christ, then learning directly from him, face to face with their Master, was a pre-requisite. Jesus schooled his disciples through a warm and challenging relationship, as we shall see in the next chapter.

So Jesus' teaching had huge impact, reaching the hearts of many, and it was also very wise, employing various communication strategies. Now let us examine a third aspect of his teaching.

Profound and coherent
So far, we have seen aspects of *how* Jesus taught. Now we shall analyse *what* he taught. This is not the place to consider the message of Jesus in itself, but we certainly need to focus our attention briefly on the structure and coherence, the directional narrative thread of his teachings, an important

indicator of his mental health and moral rectitude. It would correspond to what we call in psychiatry the *content* of one's thoughts. Jesus' discourse was coherent, profound and morally irreproachable. We could say that it was extraordinary in its most literal sense: it went beyond any ordinary ethical message.

This coherence and depth can be better understood if we group his teachings into three main areas. These correlate with the threefold relationships of human beings, namely with ourselves, with others and with God. Jesus showed an unusually profound perception in these three, and his teaching has provided us with unsurpassable wisdom and challenges at the same time:

1. on human nature, a radical moral diagnosis: the need to tell yourself the truth;
2. on human relationships, a radical social concern: the need to be 'salt and light';
3. on the kingdom of God, a radical spiritual challenge: the need for repentance.

On human nature: the need to tell yourself the truth
Jesus made a radical moral diagnosis.

He taught that the root of all evil lies within us. According to him, it is our unclean, poisoned hearts that make an unclean, poisoned society. He explained in plain terms the reason why there is so much trouble in this world:

> What comes out of a person is what defiles them. For it is from within, out of a person's heart, that evil thoughts come – sexual immorality, theft, murder, adultery, greed, malice, deceit, lewdness, envy, slander, arrogance and folly. All these evils come from inside and defile a person.
> (Mark 7:20–23)

For this reason, the first 'basic lesson' in Jesus' teaching had to do with self-perception, the need to open your eyes and tell yourself the truth about your own nature. Jesus showed an amazing insight into the self-deceiving mechanisms of the human mind and heart. He emphatically warned, 'Why do you look at the speck of sawdust in your brother's eye and pay no attention to the plank in your own eye?' (Luke 6:41). He wanted his hearers to realize that spoiled soil (the heart) can produce only bad, toxic seeds. This is why he started his preaching and teaching with the need to be willing to see 'the plank in your own eye'. Our moral condition is our first problem, and therefore the first issue to be solved.

His teaching was a source of truth, and his challenge was to tell yourself the truth.

On human relationships: the need to be 'salt and light'
Jesus called for radical social concern.

Jesus never aimed at a political career, and indeed deliberately renounced it (John 6:15). This is why his teaching was not political. Jesus never intended to be a Gandhi figure. His sharp answer to the question of whether or not the Jews should pay tribute to Caesar – 'Give back to Caesar what is Caesar's and to God what is God's' (Mark 12:17) – definitely removes him from the category of a freedom fighter. He certainly taught about freedom, but it was a different kind of freedom, a freedom that had to do with the claims on himself, as we will consider later.

Nevertheless, Jesus' teaching on human relationships was so deep and rich that he is considered one of the greatest moral teachers in history. His revolutionary view on love, as we saw, has shaped the ethics of millions of people through the centuries.

The crowning example of this is in the Sermon on the Mount. Considered to be one of the all-time peaks of human ethics, its wealth is attested to by believers and non-believers alike. As Malcolm Muggeridge said,

> No words ever uttered, it is safe to say, have had anything like the impact of these . . . Christ turned the world's accepted standards upside down. It was the poor, not the rich, who were blessed; the weak, not the strong who were to be esteemed; the pure in heart, not the sophisticated and the worldly who understood what life was about. Righteousness, not power or money, or sensual pleasures, should be man's pursuit. We should love our enemies, bless them that curse us, do good to them that hate us and pray for them that spitefully use us.[5]

The Sermon on the Mount is also considered to be a mine of mental health. Its enormous wealth is reflected upon by the psychiatrist James T. Fisher:

> If you were to take the sum total of all the authoritative articles ever written by the most qualified psychologists and psychiatrists on the subject of mental hygiene, if you were to combine them and refine them and cleave out all the excess verbiage, if you were to take the whole of the meat and none of the parsley, and if you were to have these unadulterated bits of pure scientific knowledge concisely expressed by the most capable of living poets, you would have an awkward and incomplete summation of the Sermon on the Mount.[6]

His teaching was a source of justice and dignity; his challenge was for us to be salt and light.[7]

On the kingdom of God: the need for repentance
Jesus challenged us to a radical spiritual change.

The core of Jesus' teaching was not the 'here and now', but the relationship with God and eternal life. Spiritual and moral issues were his primary concern. He certainly had a lot to say about relationships and social problems, but social ethics were not the essence of his message. The kingdom of God occupied a central place in his preaching from the very beginning, as Matthew clearly indicates: 'Jesus began to preach, "Repent, for the kingdom of heaven has come near . . ." Jesus went throughout Galilee, teaching in their synagogues, proclaiming the good news of the kingdom' (Matthew 4:17, 23). Likewise, many of the parables explain the elementary truths concerning the planting, development and final vindication of the kingdom of God. His teaching was a source of salvation; he challenged people to repentance and new birth.

Much more could be said about Jesus as a teacher, but one thing is quite disturbing: Jesus was constantly talking about himself; his teaching revolved all the time around himself. The claims about his identity – 'I am' – if not true, are those of a megalomaniac. As we said before, this is the clue to understanding fully the uniqueness of Jesus' life and work. (We will go back to this in detail in chapter 9.)

2. The whole-person healer: a strong desire to help

People were amazed at what Jesus said, but also at the works he performed: 'Jesus went throughout Galilee, teaching in their synagogues, proclaiming the good news of the kingdom, and healing every disease and sickness among the people' (Matthew 4:23; 9:35). From his mouth came not only wise words, but words of healing too. He was a teacher and a healer in one. There was a natural correlation between his words and his deeds. As John Stott puts it, 'In the ministry of Jesus, words and works, gospel preaching and compassionate service, went hand in hand. His works expressed his words, and his words explained his works.'[8]

If Jesus as a teacher exhibited lucid, coherent thinking, as a healer he displayed a strong desire to help and do good to others. This second indicator of mental stability is related primarily to the will and is expressed in concrete decisions. There is a volitional element – to wish for something – which is affected in mental disorders. Apathy, lack of desire and weak will-power are frequent symptoms of many emotional problems.

Jesus himself explicitly mentioned this close relationship between 'wish for' and 'healing' when he cured a leper:

> A man with leprosy came and knelt before him and said, 'Lord, if you are willing, you can make me clean.'
>
> Jesus reached out his hand and touched the man. 'I am willing,' he said. 'Be clean!' Immediately he was cleansed of his leprosy.
> (Matthew 8:2–3)

We know that Jesus had a special concern for the sick and the infirm.[9] The blind, the lepers, the lame, the epileptics, the demon-possessed were very much on Jesus' heart. It is in these acts of healing that his goodness, sensitivity, compassion and, above all, his love shine to the utmost. Jesus loved the sick because each person had immense value for him. This profound 'sense of the person' has always characterized the great physicians, experts not only in curing, but also in dealing with their patients in a kind and sympathetic manner.[10]

In his care for the whole person, Jesus was a forerunner of the modern principle of 'medicine of the person',[11] which concerns itself equally with the sufferer as well as the illness. He sought to heal not only the body, but also the entire person, including emotional, moral and spiritual problems. For example, to the paralysed man in Capernaum, he not only said, 'Get up, take your mat and go home', but also, 'Take heart, son; your sins are forgiven' (Matthew 9:1–6). Jesus knew very well the close relationship between body, mind and spirit, and their influence on a person's health.

The reaction of people before such a 'great physician' is not surprising: 'Many who heard him were astonished, saying, " . . . What is the wisdom given to him? What mighty works are wrought by his hands!"' (Mark 6:2, RSV). Similarly, when the Gerasene demon-possessed man was restored, 'the man went away and began to tell in the Decapolis how much Jesus had done for him. And all the people were amazed' (Mark 5:20).

Notice also the wide spectrum of this healing ministry. His care was not only for the whole person, but for all kinds of people wherever he went: 'He went about all Galilee . . . So his fame spread throughout all Syria, and they brought him all the sick, those afflicted with various diseases and pains, demoniacs, epileptics, and paralytics, and he healed them' (Matthew 4:23–24, RSV). His constant travelling was due to his sense of mission, the clear purpose, mentioned earlier. He said several times, 'It is necessary for me to go . . .' Jesus' deep concern for the sick and for 'all the weary and heavy laden' was not merely social or humanitarian. For him, the fight against sickness and disease formed a part of the coming of the kingdom of God to this earth. The healing miracles were supernatural demonstrations of this kingdom.

A strong desire to help and heal is the mark of a good person and a mature character. For this reason, Jesus' incessant healing activity communicates an eloquent message regarding his moral goodness as well as his mental strength and stability.

3. The restorer of marginalized lives: a warm heart

One of the most attractive facets of Jesus' life is his utter identification with the outcast. He once said, 'It is not the healthy who need a doctor, but those who are ill. But go and learn what this means: "I desire mercy, not sacrifice. For I have not come to call the righteous, but sinners"' (Matthew 9:12–13). Who were these 'sick' and these 'sinners'? Very different kinds of people with a common feature: they were all rejected by society:

- tax collectors and prostitutes, rejected because of their behaviour;
- lepers, rejected because of their sickness;
- women, children and the poor, rejected because of their status.

His warm and compassionate heart was very sensitive to the most vulnerable ones in a class-ridden society that was prone to rejecting those who did not fulfil their criteria of 'normality'. Jesus was not only a great physician, but also a great restorer; indeed, he rebuilt many broken lives, lives that were without dignity and purpose in the eyes of others. The oppressed and marginalized, the feeble and the lonely, those wandering in the deserts of life, were all recipients of his care and concern. Even non-Christians admire this 'social sensitivity' of Jesus.

Jesus always treated these 'second-class' human beings in a gracious, courteous way, raising their dignity as individuals to its fullest expression. What does this attitude reveal? Jesus as a restorer of broken lives bears witness to two of his essential traits: his pastoral heart and his sense of justice. Both are a strong evidence of mental health and moral goodness.

A pastoral heart

'When he saw the crowds, he had compassion on them, because they were harassed and helpless, like sheep without a shepherd' (Matthew 9:36). Jesus frequently employed the figure of the good shepherd to refer to his life of service: 'I am the good shepherd; I know my sheep' (John 10:14). The tender heart of the good shepherd is what leads him to identify with the weak sheep, those in need, the lost ones, as the prophet Isaiah anticipated:

> He tends his flock like a shepherd:
>   he gathers the lambs in his arms
> and carries them close to his heart;
>   he gently leads those that have young.
> (Isaiah 40:11)

The good shepherd 'knows his sheep' (John 10:14) and has a great capacity for understanding them. This virtue, called 'empathy', is again a reliable indicator of emotional health. The words and behaviour of a mentally unstable person usually express difficulty in empathy. The greater the mental disturbance, the greater the lack of empathy will be. Psychopathy is the maximal expression of this condition; we see this to a lesser degree in paranoia and in various other personality disorders.

The tender heart of the good shepherd surrounds the whole of the ministry and life of Jesus: it was poured out to every person he encountered and in every deed he performed.

A profound sense of justice

'Blessed are those who thirst and hunger for righteousness' (Matthew 5:6). While in his healings Jesus shows his great sense of the person, in his compassionate solidarity with the marginalized he unfolds his profound sense of justice. It was this sense of justice that went hand in hand with his hatred of sin, conflict and oppression. Indeed, love and justice are inseparable in Jesus' life. His message is good news not only of love, but also of justice. 'Blessed are those who thirst and hunger for righteousness,' he clearly taught in the Beatitudes (Matthew 5:6).

Notice how Jesus finishes the controversy at Matthew's house: 'But go and learn what this means: "I desire mercy, not sacrifice"' (Matthew 9:13). He did not limit righteousness to a private and personal matter, but rather it included social righteousness. This is why his hatred of sin always went alongside his being 'a friend of sinners'.

In summary, here we have someone with a coherent and profound message, an admired teacher; an individual with deep empathy and sympathy for the sick, the healer of the whole person; a man whose tender heart for the oppressed and the marginalized aroused the hostility of the establishment. Would anyone dare to deny that this selfless and powerful exercise of gifts reveals an exceptionally stable character and an unsurpassable goodness? No mentally sick person, no evil man, would ever have been able to speak or behave in the impeccable and influential way that Jesus did. In our opinion, the evidence is again convincing: Jesus was not only a man with a balanced personality, but he also lived a totally righteous life. If his character makes him attractive, his words and deeds make him unique. We find no discrepancy between his being and his doing. The words and deeds of Jesus plainly indicate extraordinary mental health and unequivocal moral uprightness.

When John the Baptist was in prison, he began to doubt the identity of Jesus: 'Are you the one who is to come, or should we expect someone else?' (Luke 7:19). Jesus responded by pointing to the objective evidence, all his extraordinary deeds and words, and in doing so, he gave an excellent résumé of his life: 'Go back and report to John what you have seen and heard: the blind receive sight, the lame walk, those who have leprosy are cleansed, the deaf hear, the dead are raised, and the good news is proclaimed to the poor' (Luke 7:22).

This comprehensive response dissipated all the doubts of the imprisoned prophet. And his last words to John are a gentle but decisive challenge to us all: 'Blessed is anyone who does not stumble on account of me' (Luke 7:23).

6. THE TEST OF RELATIONSHIPS: 'HAVING LOVED HIS OWN . . . HE LOVED THEM TO THE END'

Good health consists not only of a fit body or a balanced mind, but also of harmonious relationships.[1] Personal relationships constitute an excellent test of maturity. They are like character X-rays that enhance both virtues and defects. Think, for example, of someone who has had a positive and lasting influence on your life. Most likely, this person was on good terms with himself or herself, and subsequently was on good terms with you. In my case, I (Pablo) will never forget the example of John Stott.[2] He had an incredible capacity for friendship, to the point that he was known as 'Uncle John' all over the world. I have never met anyone with a similar gift for making friends. As a radical disciple of Jesus, his inner peace and joy were reflected in the very affable, affectionate way in which he related to others.

The ability to establish solid and stable connections, to have and maintain friendships, to love and give oneself to a neighbour, is a very reliable indicator of both emotional health and moral goodness. It is in our relationships with others that the best and worst in us are revealed. This is especially true in our closest relationships, those that require commitment and loyalty, surrender and self-giving, the capacity to accept and to forgive: in a nutshell, where the emotional balance and moral quality of a person are both put to the test. As a matter of fact, a deep disturbance in the ability to start or maintain relationships is a component in most psychiatric disorders.

In the last chapter we considered how Jesus related to crowds – his public life; now we will explore how he related to individuals and to a small group – his private life. These relationships give us deeper insight, and important clues in evaluating both his mental stability and his moral goodness. At the same time they help us to understand the extraordinary influence he had on people. We will analyse later (in chapter 8) the transforming power of Jesus, but here his relationships will provide us with an initial glimpse of his unique capacity to change lives.

Encounters that transformed lives: some observations

We know by now that Jesus was profoundly relational. What can we discover by looking at his relationships? He interacted with all kinds of people, building strong connections where unconditional love, trust, faithfulness, compassion and grace were paramount. As we have already seen, Jesus was not only an admired teacher and a much sought-after healer, he was a friend of women and children, the poor and outcast, tax collectors and sinners, Samaritans and Gentiles. Jesus was not a distant public figure, avoiding contact with his audience. Many times we read that 'he drew near to people' or 'the people came near to him'. To be close to people and available to meet their needs was his concern. And Jesus never used people; he served them.

Nevertheless, the defining feature of Jesus' relationships was not affection or compassion, but transformation. The main outcome was not feeling loved, but being changed by him. In the Gospel narratives we find striking examples of individuals whose lives were transformed through an encounter with Jesus. They were very different characters, but with one thing in common: they had all experienced some sort of void in their lives. Jesus transformed their empty existence into a life of fullness and purpose.

This was the case with Zacchaeus, a greedy tax collector for whom money was not enough. The encounter with Jesus changed him into a generous giver (Luke 19:1–10). A similar experience was that of Nicodemus, the unsatisfied theologian for whom religion was not enough. His meeting with Jesus changed his hollow religion into true faith (John 3:1–21). He was eventually one of the two men who helped in the burial of Jesus (John 19:39). Both Zacchaeus and Nicodemus experienced the deeply transforming power of Jesus. The change reached every area of their life: identity, behaviour, values and relationships. They fully experienced what he claimed: 'I have come that they may have life, and have it to the full' (John 10:10).

For the rest of this chapter we will focus on two encounters that are highlights in the relationships of Jesus. First, the personal encounter with the Samaritan woman, which provides us with an excellent summary of both his character and the way he treated everyone as a human being. Then the relationship of the Master with his disciples, a group encounter, where we see his stature as a leader.

Jesus and the Samaritan woman: loneliness and marginalization changed into fullness of life
(John 4:5–42)

It was a hot summer's day when Jesus stopped with his disciples beside a well in the region of Samaria. There was no-one around except a woman. The disciples went off to the closest village to buy food. Probably John remained with the Master. They would not have left him alone, especially in that place. In this simple, everyday setting Jesus has one of his most significant encounters. What stands out is his extra-ordinary ability to reach and meet the woman's deepest needs. The result was complete transformation.

The troubles of a marginalized woman

Here we have a woman who goes to draw water at midday, when the sun and heat are at their peak and no-one else is out and about. This detail gives us an important indication of her personal situation. Why does she go out at this hour when everyone else is at home avoiding the heat? She wants to remain unnoticed; she doesn't want her neighbours to see her. There is some reason for the uneasiness in her life that causes her to isolate herself.

This woman had three reasons to feel marginalized: she was a woman (gender prejudice), she was Samaritan (ethnic discrimination) and she was a sinner, now co-habiting with a man to whom she was not married (moral compromise). Consequently, the portrait of the Samaritan woman reveals a situation where social, relational and moral issues are interconnected. Loneliness, shame and marginal-ization form the background of such a portrait. Here we have a needy human being whose life seems empty and meaningless.

What does Jesus do in this situation? How does he treat the woman? This story points to the radical nature of Jesus in two practical ways: in relation to tradition, he breached social conventions; in relation to the woman, he reached out to her deepest needs. As mentioned earlier, to be a radical is not the same as to be an extremist. For Jesus, radicalism meant getting to the root of a problem or situation. Here we witness how he was able to accomplish this.

Jesus breaches social conventions

First of all, Jesus was radical in that he broke with the traditions and prejudices of the day. For him, the person came first. Social labels and the pressure of tradition did not prevent him from treating this woman as a human being. As a result, he took the initiative in the conversation: 'When a Samaritan woman came to draw water, Jesus said to her, "Will you give me a drink?"' (John 4:7). It was not proper in that culture for a man to speak with a woman in public, and the disciples were naturally perplexed: 'Just then his disciples returned and were surprised to find him talking with a woman. But no one asked, "What do you want?" or "Why are you talking with her?"' (4:27). Moreover, she was a Samaritan, so she was surprised that Jesus, a Jewish man, would even speak to her: 'The Samaritan woman said to him, "You are a Jew and I am a Samaritan woman. How can you ask me for a drink?" (For Jews do not associate with Samaritans.)' (4:9).

Jesus took the first step by talking with her. This underscores two virtues of his character. On the one hand, we see his courage. Jesus was never concerned about being 'politically correct'. He was above any form of prejudice or social convention. He was in no way a narcissist seeking to please everyone, or a coward incapable of confronting rules and tradition. Jesus had the boldness to ignore social and cultural paradigms whenever it was necessary.

On the other hand, Jesus' attitude towards the Samaritan woman reveals a deep love for her as a person; he behaves with sensitivity and empathy, especially towards those who are weaker, in this case, a woman. Jesus cared for women, treating them with love and tenderness, restoring their dignity and thus opening the door for a real breakthrough in the equality of all human beings, regardless of their gender.

Such a caring and honouring attitude is recorded time and again in the Gospels, especially by Luke, the doctor. Jesus related to women in a courteous and natural way, never with hostility, and he was at ease in their company. No psychological barriers or conflict arose in his relationships with them, but rather the opposite: they felt understood, affirmed and unconditionally loved by him.

Indeed, from his birth to his death Jesus allowed women to play a significant role in his ministry. His most intimate circle of friends included Mary and Martha, the sisters of Lazarus, in whose home he spent many hours of rest. Then there were other loyal women alongside him until his death on the cross. His example remains a shining light in the darkness of a society where using and abusing women was sadly a constant reality. In the way Jesus treated children and women we see one of the most singular and eloquent evidences of his emotional well-being and moral stature.

Jesus reaches to the root of her problem

Secondly, Jesus was radical in his ability to reach the depths of the human soul. The woman's marginalization was due not only to social factors (being a woman or being poor) or to her ethnicity (a Samaritan). She had a deeper problem, one connected with her moral and spiritual life. Most likely, she was not aware of its importance; this is why 'Jesus awakened in her higher thoughts, and pointed her to spiritual and eternal realities'.[3]

The ensuing dialogue is fascinating, because in it we see all the levels of human communication. We find simple words of courtesy, an exchange of ideas on religion and rites, culminating in a sharing of feelings and her most intimate life. Jesus proves himself to be a master in the art of conversation, leading the woman to the level of insight she needs in order to see and understand her problem:

> 'Go, call your husband and come back.'
>
> 'I have no husband,' she replied.
>
> Jesus said to her, 'You are right when you say you have no husband. The fact is, you have had five husbands, and the man you now have is not your husband. What you have just said is quite true.'
>
> (John 4:16–18)

These key words of Jesus opened her eyes. At the right moment in the discussion, the Master confronts her with her past and her present, provoking a quick life revision. After having had five husbands, she now cohabits with a man without being married to him. We do not know why she has had five husbands: she could have been a widow or she could have been divorced. In both situations there is a history of grief and pain. The deep perception of Jesus led the woman right to the core of her problem. The real issue was not a religious one, nor a social or an emotional one; the ultimate source of her emptiness was an ethical and spiritual one. Certainly social problems affected her, but the main disturbance came not from outside, but from inside her; the origin of her troubles was not social, but biographical. The main reason why she marvelled at his words was because he 'told me everything I've ever done' (verse 29).

A radical diagnosis brings forth a radical change

The radical attitude of Jesus to reach out to the heart of the problem produces an immediate and very visible effect on the woman: 'Then, leaving her water jar, the woman went back to the town and said to the people, "Come, see a man who told me everything I've ever done. Could this be the Messiah?"' (John 4:28–29).

'She left . . . she went back . . . she said.' The dramatic change in the marginalized and empty life of the Samaritan woman is magnificently portrayed in these three verbs. Her priorities changed, her relationships changed and her 'message' changed. Before, she hid herself so as not to be seen; now, she goes in search of people in the town. Before she merely survived; now she shares her joy of living. Before she kept quiet; now she enthusiastically retells her story. Her shame and isolation have been transformed into joy.

Her change is measurable: everyone in the village can see it. Her message is unquestionable: 'He told me everything I've ever done' (4:39). She has experienced deep personal change. So sincere are her words and so convincing the change brought about in her life that 'Many of the Samaritans from that town believed in him because of the woman's testimony'. An encounter with Jesus transformed her life and theirs for ever.

We also need to make reference to one key issue in the narrative. Jesus, for the first time according to John, openly declares his divine identity: 'The woman said, "I know that Messiah" (called Christ) "is coming. When he comes, he will explain everything to us." Then Jesus declared, "I, the one speaking to you – I am he"' (4:25–26). This is the first 'I am' declaration of Jesus whereby he indicates that he is equal to God. Several more would follow, making clear his unequivocal claim to be God.

We must now ask ourselves, does Jesus exhibit any sign of mental disorder in this narrative? An impartial answer obliges us to recognize not only the absence of any pathology, but also his extraordinary capacity to relate to others, to love them and to influence their lives for good. These are the traits of someone who is well balanced and morally good.

We move now from a *personal* encounter to a *group* encounter. Relationships must be tested at both levels. Let us see how the Jesus admired by the multitudes and loved by individuals also inspired deep affection and closeness in his small group of disciples. Transformation, a profound life change, was the final outcome here too.

Jesus and the disciples: fishermen changed into preachers and teachers

The private life of Jesus is at stake here. The test of relationships reaches its maximum level of difficulty because living together for three years with a very mixed group indeed constitutes a sharp character X-ray! Life in a group is incompatible with individualism and egotism; it implies adaptation and acceptance, flexibility and renunciation, solidarity and generosity. Indeed, living in community is like taking an exam in patience, comprehension and love, all at the same time. It is in the context of close relationships that levels of affection and emotional intimacy arise, but also conflict and tension, because we become more exposed and vulnerable.

Jesus' relationship with his twelve disciples provides us with a superb portrait of his capacity also to relate on good terms with a group. We discover here the stability and maturity of Jesus, 'the healthiest mind of all', through three features:

1. the calling: his moral authority
2. the transformation: his modelling leadership
3. the provision: his integral care.

1. The calling: his moral authority

The disciples 'left everything and followed him' (Luke 5:11). Here was an authority based on attraction and trust. Jesus takes the initiative to form the group. First, there were two pairs of brothers, all of them fishermen: Simon Peter and Andrew, James and John (Simon Peter's partners). 'Then Jesus said to Simon, "Don't be afraid; from now on you will fish for people." So they pulled their boats up on shore, left everything and followed him' (Luke 5:10–11). It is remarkable how quickly they made the decision to leave everything and follow him (see also Matthew 4:22).

Matthew (Levi), a tax collector, had a very similar experience: 'After this, Jesus went out and saw a tax collector by the name of Levi sitting at his tax booth. "Follow me," Jesus said to him, and Levi got up, left everything and followed him' (Luke 5:27–28). We have referred to trust several times as a key theme in speaking of Jesus. The story of Matthew and the calling of the disciples help us to understand it better. How can we explain their immense trust in a person whom they hardly knew, the kind of trust that compelled them to leave everything and follow him? From the very beginning Jesus radiated great authority. It was not the authority that comes from a position of power – a simple command, giving orders – but the moral authority emanating from a fully trustworthy person. Such authority is not imposed; it is earned. It resorts not to obligation, but to conviction. It is an authority related to attraction, the power to draw others to oneself.

Jesus wanted followers not by obligation but by identification, not forced into service, but serving from the heart. This principle remained until the end of his life, and it is still fully valid today: following Jesus is a matter not of obligation but of attraction. His authority is not that of a despot who gives orders, but that of a lover who attracts with moral beauty.

This is the reason why the apostles followed him 'at once', without any hesitation. There was something special about the 'Master from Galilee' that dissipated any doubt as to his credibility. As we said earlier, they soon realized that Jesus was a fully trustworthy person.

Jesus is not afraid of diversity. He forms a group that is strikingly heterogeneous in many ways. It wasn't an easy group! Sooner or later there would be tensions. Among the Twelve there are fishermen and tax collectors, from nationalists to collaborators with the Empire, from impulsive to melancholic temperaments. It seems that Jesus was interested in bringing together a broad representation of cultural, social, professional and temperamental backgrounds. Why? Wouldn't it have been much easier working with a more homogeneous group?

The Master was a powerful cohesive factor in the equation. This surprising and deliberate diversity tells us something about Jesus' unique ability to bring cohesion to the group. He wasn't at all afraid to lead a group that could potentially flare up in conflict because of its diversity. His very presence was a strong stabilizing factor. Jesus was completely the opposite of a toxic person whose mere presence curdles the atmosphere within a group.

Additionally, when conflict did arise, Jesus is seen as a formidable psychologist, an expert in group dynamics. There were certainly tense moments in their relationships: jealousy, personal ambitions and even open betrayal reared their ugly heads, but Jesus handled the conflicts expertly and deactivated all the 'bombs' that could blow up the group. Their time together was a lesson in coexistence in preparation for a greater purpose. No wonder that strong bonds were developed among them, to such an extent that shortly before Jesus' death Peter said to Jesus, 'Lord, why can't I follow you now? I will lay down my life for you' (John 13:37).

2. The transformation: his modelling leadership

'When they saw the courage of Peter and John and realised that they were unschooled, ordinary men, they were astonished and they took note that these men had been with Jesus' (Acts 4:13). Jesus' moral authority was endorsed by the way he modelled leadership. This second feature will confirm once more his unique character and healthy mind. The figure of Jesus as a leader shines brightly in his daily relationship with the disciples. Jesus not only knew how to relate well to a group, but he himself created, modelled and led it from beginning to end. The complete transformation of this heterogeneous group is a fascinating process.

What could be expected from this tiny band of followers? These simple men selected by Jesus, most of them uneducated, did not bode well for a very bright future. What happened? What strange process caused such apparently poor human capital to become so profoundly changed?

We read that 'Jesus went up on a mountainside and called to him those he wanted, and they came to him. He appointed twelve *that they might be with him* and that he might send them out to preach' (Mark 3:13–14, italics mine). Learning was through example: 'that they might be with him'. How did Jesus mould these men so that the religious leaders in

Jerusalem 'were astonished'? The words of Acts 4:13, quoted above, give us the clue: 'and they took note that these men had been with Jesus'.

Jesus was a model for them to imitate. There is a kind of learning that can be gained only through example, by living daily together. This is learning through imitation and identification. In order to become like someone else, a close-up model is needed. Following the inaugural lesson known as 'The Mission of the Twelve' (Mark 6:7–13, RSV), the apostles learned not only from Jesus' words, but also from his reactions, from his attitudes, from his way of resting, and also of praying, in short, from his entire way of being. They learned from the way he treated them and others: 'He bore patiently with laziness, ignorance, fear and failure, and never gave up on his disciples. He challenged, confronted and corrected.'[4]

3. The provision: his integral care

'I am the good shepherd. The good shepherd lays down his life for the sheep,' we read in John 10:11. Jesus was not a theoretical teacher in an ivory tower. He never neglected daily provision for his disciples, whether material, emotional or spiritual. This third feature reveals a balanced and integral leadership, very far removed from insanity or extremism.

Jesus cared for their material needs
Jesus' great spirituality made him deeply human. The Master did not concern himself with only the strategic and spiritual aspects of the disciples' task. Notice, for example, how in his mission instructions he gave them a series of guidelines that demonstrated a very practical sense of reality.

He cared that the disciples should have adequate rest. Thus, on several occasions we see Jesus taking the Twelve to a quiet place, far from the multitude, to renew their strength. He also cared about food, as is evident in the miracles of feeding the multitudes. Nourishing the body was important for Jesus to the extent that he included 'our daily bread' as one of the basic petitions in his model prayer, known as 'Our Father'.

Jesus oversaw their emotional and spiritual needs

Jesus was also concerned about the emotional needs of the group. Striking evidence of his care is shown in the way in which he prepared the apostles for their separation from him. Remarkably, there were two very significant moments of in-depth teaching in the school of Christ: at the beginning and at the end of his ministry. Once again, the wisdom of Jesus as a leader surfaces: it is important to start well, but it is even more important to end well. That's why, just before he is betrayed and handed over, Jesus gives his final lessons in both word and deed.

Memorable final lessons

The lessons of Jesus' 'intensive course' contain some of his most beautiful words and deeds.[5] Above all, they show us his matchless moral stature. The attractiveness of Jesus reaches its maximum splendour in these moments of intimacy with the apostles in the days before his death.

'I loved you. Now remain in my love' (John 15:9). John's narrative begins by framing all that is going to follow: 'It was just before the Passover Festival. Jesus knew that the hour had come for him to leave this world and go to the Father. Having loved his own who were in the world, he loved them to the end' (John 13:1). So, first of all, Jesus reiterates his love to them. They had enjoyed a close-knit relationship, full of affection and emotional warmth. Jesus loved them and now he openly tells them so: 'As the Father has loved me, so have I loved you. Now remain in my love' (15:9).

Preparing for bereavement: 'You have loved me.' Love and trust were the foundation on which their community life was based. This is why Jesus goes on to call them friends: 'You are my friends . . . I no longer call you servants, because a servant does not know his master's business. Instead, I have called you friends, for everything that I learned from my Father I have made known to you' (John 15:14–15). In this emotional crescendo Jesus implies that he has felt loved by them: 'you have loved me' (16:27). This expression of mutual love is an excellent preparation for their approaching bereavement; the pain of their loss will be relieved because, in a sense, they 'have done their homework'.

Preparing for mission: 'You must love one another.' Jesus' words, however, are more than a declaration of mutual affection with emotionally therapeutic purposes. His key intention continues to be to teach the disciples regarding their future responsibility. Hence his passionate exhortation: 'A new command I give you: love one another. As I have loved you, so you must love one another. By this everyone will know that you are my disciples, if you love one another' (John 13:34–35).

Giving hope: 'I will see you again.' This emotional and spiritual preparation culminates in something even more essential: hope. Jesus knew very well that hope is to life what oxygen is to the lungs. That is why he gives them hope: 'Now is your time of grief, but I will see you again and you will rejoice, and no one will take away your joy' (16:22). He comforts them with these words:

> Do not let your hearts be troubled . . . My Father's house has many rooms; if that were not so, would I have told you that I am going there to prepare a place for you? And if I go and

prepare a place for you, I will come back and take you
to be with me that you also may be where I am.
(John 14:1–3)

A wise and calm reply in the face of adversity defines a good
leader. A final lesson was still missing in this 'intensive course'.
Two episodes of great emotional intensity reveal to us the
self-control of Jesus and his skill as a leader: the announcement
of Judas' mortal treason (13:21–30) and the forewarning of
Peter's denial (13:36–38). We will consider them in greater
detail in the next chapter. Suffice it to say now that the Last
Supper could well have ended in drama, with the group
breaking up and fighting among themselves, except for the
fact that their leader was also a master in forgiveness and in
the business of restoring the fallen.

The closing prayer: an open window into the heart of Jesus.
The 'intensive course' ends with a prayer. Jesus' care for the
disciples culminates with the paramount resource: intercession
before the Father.

In his prayer (John 17), the traits of the good shepherd –
the leader par excellence – flow powerfully. He prays for
protection, provision, growth and love. A formidable summary of emotional intelligence and pastoral care! Once again
he gives us a glimpse of his matchless goodness and love,
without the least hint of wrongdoing, egotism or imbalance.

So the transformation of this handful of men, humanly
weak and limited, was so complete that 'Day after day, in the
temple courts and from house to house, they never stopped
teaching and proclaiming the good news that Jesus is
the Messiah' (Acts 5:42). And 'they were highly regarded
by the people' (Acts 5:13). Of them it was said that they
'turned the world upside down' (Acts 17:6, RSV). A true meta-
morphosis had occurred that couldn't be explained merely

by way of educational or psychological methods. Jesus had planted seeds in their hearts that a greater force had caused to germinate in a supernatural way. This force transformed their weakness into strength, their ignorance into wisdom, their cowardice into bravery, their poverty into riches. A personal encounter with Jesus changed everything.

We said at the beginning of this chapter that personal relationships constitute an important test of maturity. Now we are in a position to say that Jesus has passed this test with flying colours. Relationships were so paramount in his life that the last words he spoke on earth were words of relationship, a promise of being with his own always: 'And surely I am with you always, to the very end of the age' (Matthew 28:20).

7. THE TEST OF ADVERSITY: 'THEREFORE HAVE I SET MY FACE LIKE FLINT . . .'

A man's value is to be measured not so much by his successes, as by the way he takes his failures.
Paul Tournier

Someone's reaction in the face of adversity demonstrates the true measure of that person. It is in the hour of trial that the maturity of our character and our mental strength are put to the test. We admire and are greatly inspired when we consider, for example, the life stories of disabled athletes who overcame adversity and turned it into success.

Jason Lester was hit by a car when he was twelve years old and he suffered a paralysed arm. Years later he became a world-class ultra-endurance sports champion. Today he can swim powerfully, and cycle and run long distances – all without the full use of his right arm. In 2009 he was awarded 'Best Male Athlete with a Disability' and became the first male triathlete to win such an honour. In his autobiography *Running on Faith*, he tells of his rise to fame and how he relied on God in the face of adversity.

How do we face the tough times? It is easy to run with the wind at our back, but our real strength is tested when we have it in our face. So far we have seen Jesus mainly as a man of 'success', admired as a public figure and loved by his friends. The relationships with his followers have demonstrated some very positive facets. The picture, however, would not be complete if we did not consider also how the Master acted and reacted before his opponents, those who drove him to death. The relationship with his enemies and his reaction to adversity form an essential test to corroborate or refute what we have seen of Jesus so far.

So how did Jesus react in the hour of his life storms? Some of the character traits that we considered in chapter 4 shine powerfully as he approaches death: acceptance expressed in serenity; patience expressed in strength of spirit; courage expressed in determination; meekness expressed in self-control. This was his response to adversity and injustice: a superb lesson in maturity and mental strength.

Moments of composure in the face of pressure

It was on his way to martyrdom that Jesus wrote the most beautiful pages of his life's book, pages abounding in powerful silent messages. In fact, these messages were so eloquent in themselves that words were unnecessary. We will consider four of these key episodes in the ordeal of Jesus, where the most accurate portrait of his character is revealed and where he showed 'the greatest composure under pressure':[1]

1. facing the pain caused by your own: Judas and Peter
2. agony in the garden: a night-watch 'with loud cries and tears'
3. a shameful judgment in the court of (in)justice
4. 'the seven words from the cross': Jesus' supreme sermon.

1. Facing the pain caused by your own: Judas and Peter

'They say that betrayal cuts deeper than any other kind of pain. Probably that's because only a friend can betray you. An enemy can't . . . Judas, someone from the Lord's inner circle of closest friends, stabbed him in the back,'[2] said Joni Eareckson Tada.

The most painful wounds are those caused by your loved ones, your friends. This is especially true if they fail you when you need them, in the time of adversity. You expect their company and support, but instead you find disloyalty and betrayal. This was exactly Jesus' experience with two of his disciples. Judas betrayed him treacherously and handed him over to death. Peter denied him three times, leaving Jesus alone when he most needed the warm support of a friend.

The way Jesus reacted to the ingratitude and disloyalty of his own reveals key aspects of his character: serenity, self-control and agape love. The case of Peter, furthermore, provides us with a practical lesson in how to restore the fallen.

Judas' betrayal: the kiss of the traitor

Jesus and his disciples are celebrating the Last Supper, a time of intimacy and deep significance for the group. Suddenly the Master announces the betrayal. John, an eyewitness to the facts, describes with the perception of a psychologist something of Jesus' state of mind at this moment: 'After he had said this, Jesus was troubled in spirit and testified, "Very truly I tell you, one of you is going to betray me"' (John 13:21).

Jesus cannot avoid feeling deeply disturbed. The expression 'was troubled in spirit' is the same as the one used for the intense grief of Jesus at the tomb of Lazarus. Deeply troubled, indeed, but there is no mention of anger or resentment. Jesus could have expelled Judas from that communion table.

Shouting a vigorous 'get out of here' would have been quite understandable. Judas' presence was highly disruptive in such an intimate atmosphere. Jesus, however, did not cast him out; it was Judas who parted from them once the supper had finished.

Deeply disturbed, yet deeply merciful, Jesus responds to the traitor with grace and love. What an amazing way to react! He practised what he preached: love your enemy. We see this unique reaction again in the very moment of the betrayal: 'Going at once to Jesus, Judas said, "Greetings, Rabbi!" and kissed him. Jesus replied, "Do what you came for, friend." Then the men stepped forward, seized Jesus and arrested him' (Matthew 26:48–50).

The traitor is called 'friend'. It is impressive to see Jesus addressing Judas in this way. The most natural reaction would have been defence, reproach or even revenge for so great an outrage. You need to be very strong psychologically to respond to the treachery of one of your own with the self-control of Jesus, but still greater is the moral integrity that leads him to respond to so much wickedness with grace and love. Notice the contrast with the disciples' reaction: 'When Jesus' followers saw what was going to happen, they said, "Lord, should we strike with our swords?"' (Luke 22:49).

The impulsive Peter drew his sword and struck one of the soldiers (verse 50). The immediate response of Jesus is: '"No more of this!" And he touched the man's ear and healed him' (verse 51). Even in this moment of utmost tribulation he is concerned about healing the wound of the soldier. Jesus' only protest was that he was not leading a rebellion, but had been teaching daily at the temple. He loved Judas; he healed the soldier. Loving and healing were his hallmark until the end.

No impulsiveness, but self-control and serenity; no hatred, but love and grace; no symptoms whatsoever of low tolerance to frustration (immaturity) or cowardice. Rather, he 'set his face like flint' (Isaiah 50:7). The 'lesson without words' of Jesus reached the heart of Judas sharply like an arrow, and, 'seized with remorse', he returned the thirty pieces of silver. Then he exclaimed bitterly, 'I have sinned . . . for I have betrayed innocent blood' (Matthew 27:4). 'Innocent blood'. These words smote Judas' conscience unbearably. We know the end: the traitor took his own life; the innocent gave his own life.

Peter's denial: the disloyalty of the friend

Peter is so determined to follow Jesus to death that he boldly says, 'Lord, why can't I follow you now? I will lay down my life for you' (John 13:37). Jesus responds to this firm declaration of loyalty with a disappointing announcement: 'Will you really lay down your life for me? Very truly I tell you, before the cock crows, you will disown me three times!' (verse 38).

It happened exactly as the Master foretold. If Judas handed him over to death, Peter abandoned Jesus at the edge of death. The strong fisherman, the impulsive and determined apostle, behaved like a feeble coward. We come to discover the pain that such disloyalty caused in Jesus through a look: 'The Lord turned and looked straight at Peter. Then Peter remembered the word the Lord had spoken to him: "Before the cock crows today, you will disown me three times"' (Luke 22:61).

What a look! It was not a mere glance. It must have been an intense, penetrating look, a look of sadness and love at the same time. Campbell Morgan describes it this way: 'It was a look of penetration . . . the sense of it might be expressed by "He looked *through* him."'[3] There was pain in this gaze, grief caused by the cowardice of the friend and the disloyalty of the disciple, but we do not discern any reproach or resentment in it. At no time was Jesus 'troubled in spirit' as with Judas.

This look broke Peter's heart, so then 'he went outside and wept bitterly' (Matthew 26:75). These tears of repentance would open the door for a full restoration.

Jesus did not hesitate to restore the fallen friend. Actually, even before Peter's denial, Jesus had promised to pray for him: 'But I have prayed for you, Simon, that your faith may not fail' (Luke 22:32). This prayer surely included the specific plan the Master had to restore the feeble apostle.

So, first, Jesus pledges Peter his full support in prayer, then he 'sends' him a very special look of love, and later he takes the initiative to forgive and restore him fully (see next chapter). As with the denial, Jesus repeats his commission three times: 'Feed my sheep.' Such an expression of trust was the best balm to heal wounds that would still be raw in the apostle's heart (guilt, shame, a sense of inadequacy). Jesus restores not only his self-esteem, but above all his moral authority, a necessary step if Peter is to fulfil his responsibility as an apostle.

While through the episode of Judas's betrayal, Jesus discloses his enormous self-control and his love towards the enemy, in Peter's denial he gives us a lesson in how to treat the fallen leader: support in prayer, a look of love and an act of restoration. In both cases he shows exceptional mental strength and moral goodness.

2. Agony in the garden: a night watch 'with loud cries and tears'

Judas and Peter caused Jesus deep pain and disappointment. People can certainly be a source of trouble, but there is another kind of adversity that comes directly not from individuals, but from circumstances. In the episode that follows we will see that the disciples continued to cause frustration and grief to their Master, but, above all, we will consider how the burden of circumstances can become over-whelming, especially when it is caused by undeserved and cruel suffering.

The long hours of tension and agony in Gethsemane also reveal some key features of Jesus' character: his acceptance and courage before the ordeal, and an attitude of under-standing towards his own who fail him again. This threefold lesson will be evident to us from two prayers: a frustrated attempt to pray by the apostles, and a fervent prayer by Jesus, memorable in its form and its content. We are presented with a very special night watch, an event of great spiritual and emotional intensity. A detailed description of the context will help us capture the unique gravity and significance of these hours.

The dark night of the soul

The night before his martyrdom was long, very long, for Jesus. The events that lay ahead plunged him into deep anguish. Night was going to fall also in his soul. Why? His grief was not due simply to fear of death. Certainly an atrocious martyrdom, both physically and psychologically, was before him, but the darkness on that night lay in a more profound dimension. A fierce spiritual battle was going to be fought. His courage before the ordeal was going to be tested, yes, but above all, the test had to do with his full acceptance and submission to the will of his Father. It was the time when Isaiah's great prophecy would be fulfilled:

> Surely he took up our pain
>> and bore our suffering,
> yet we considered him punished by God,
>> stricken by him, and afflicted.
> (Isaiah 53:4)

So the intensity and extremity of the experience would go far beyond any human mental stress or suffering. This was not only a real man suffering, but God himself, in the person of his Son. With his death, the very reason for his life was at stake. The decisive hour had at last come.

A poignant portrait: 'My soul is overwhelmed with sorrow to the point of death'

How did Jesus face those hours? As we contemplate him facing his heinous death, we are deeply impressed, first of all, by the emotions in his heart. The description is a poignant one: 'He took Peter, James and John along with him, and he began to be deeply distressed and troubled. "My soul is overwhelmed with sorrow to the point of death"' (Mark 14:33–34).

The words in the original biblical text reveal a growing intensity, as the erudite Edersheim points out: 'Increasingly, with every step forward, He became "sorrowful", "full of sorrow", "sore amazed", and "desolate". This last word seems to indicate utter loneliness, desertion, and desolateness.'[4] Luke, displaying his medical knowledge, provides a revealing detail on how ominous this moment was: 'Being in anguish, he prayed more earnestly, and his sweat was like drops of blood falling to the ground' (Luke 22:44).[5] Jesus' sweat mingled with his blood, marking the climax of the intense fight he was waging.

A failed prayer: the apostles fall asleep while praying

Jesus needed prayer, a vital weapon for such a fierce contest. Therefore he seeks the support of three disciples who were very dear to him (Peter, John and James, who had shared other meaningful events with Jesus). He asks them simply, 'Stay here and keep watch with me' (Matthew 26:38). Just two requests: their company – 'stay here' – and their prayer – 'keep watch with me'. Jesus longed to feel the closeness and support of his loved ones.

What a failure! The three chosen disciples could not fulfil their Master's petition. They fell asleep, and not only once, but three times! While he lay in prayer, they lay asleep. His own had failed him again, another experience of abandonment and loneliness at the most crucial moment.

A lesson in understanding: 'The Spirit is willing but the flesh is weak'

How did Jesus react to this new disappointment with his disciples? A bad-tempered and irritable reaction would have not surprised anyone; the normal response of someone under acute stress would have been to rebuke the three sleepyheads for not being capable of supporting him. Far from that, however, he responded again not with words of reproach, but with understanding: 'The spirit is willing, but the flesh is weak' (Matthew 26:41).

Jesus was aware of the fatigue produced by the intensity of the previous hours, so draining and full of events. He understood that the apostles were emotionally and physically exhausted and their bodies required rest. What a masterly lesson in empathy!

In Gethsemane Jesus showed great strength (before his coming ordeal) and great compassion (towards the apostles). We have already seen both virtues throughout his ministry, but the unique fact here is that he displayed this unusual combination in moments of extreme tribulation, even at the very onset of torture. No circumstance, no person, nothing at all, was capable of altering his love and mercy. It can certainly be said of him that he was slow to anger and great in mercy (Psalm 103:8).

A memorable prayer: 'prayers and petitions with loud cries
and tears'
Jesus' prayer in Gethsemane is memorable, above all for its
content. What did he ask? '"*Abba*, Father," he said, "everything is possible for you. Take this cup from me. Yet not what
I will, but what you will"' (Mark 14:36).

Jesus needed to accept his imminent suffering. Acceptance,
however, is not something automatic: genuine acceptance is
a costly process requiring struggle. This is why he wrestled
in prayer. As a man, Jesus had the same reaction as any of us:
he tried to avoid the trauma and he sought to change things.
This is a legitimate and natural opposition to all kinds of
suffering. It is important, though, to notice how Jesus ends his
prayer: 'Yet not my will, but yours be done' (Luke 22:42).
Here was an obedient disposition and acceptance of his
Father's will.

Jesus' prayer impresses us also for its form, the way he
prayed. In the letter to the Hebrews we discover the emotional
intensity of Jesus' struggle in prayer: 'During the days of
Jesus' life on earth, he offered up prayers and petitions with
fervent cries and tears to the one who could save him from
death, and he was heard because of his reverent submission'
(Hebrews 5:7).

It was dark outside, but a bright light emanated from
the Master of Galilee that night. Great courage, a genuine
willingness to accept God's will and a deep empathy illuminated the darkness of an agonized night watch. Jesus' character
was shining in maximum splendour.

3. A shameful judgment in the court of (in)justice
We read, 'The chief priests and the whole Sanhedrin were
looking for evidence against Jesus so that they could put him
to death, but they did not find any' (Mark 14:55).

Jesus has now been betrayed by Judas and arrested. After the agonizing night in Gethsemane, he gets ready to face trial, a trial that unfolds in several phases. It will be a strange trial, a parody of justice. The text is very rich in details, which reveal the uniqueness of Jesus' character. What was Jesus accused of? And what did he say about himself throughout his trial? We shall consider the first question in the light of his examination before the Sanhedrin (the ecclesiastical court). The second aspect will take us before Pilate.

Crucially, finding out the reasons why his contemporaries determined to kill Jesus will give us key information about his identity, his claims and, ultimately, his mental ability.

Before Annas and Caiaphas: they were 'vehemently accusing him'

What sort of feelings does a mentally infirm person awaken in others? Does he or she annoy to the extent of provoking a desire to kill that person? If Jesus was nothing more than a 'crackpot', then why did he arouse such hostility in the Jewish religious leaders? Of what did they accuse him, in reality?

Hating a madman?

The trial before the religious authorities throws a lot of light on these questions. A person with serious mental problems, especially psychosis, awakens in others a desire to protect, not eliminate them. In psychiatry, treatment involving the use of constraint is intended to protect a patient from harming himself or herself or others. Above all, one seeks to help; in the worst of cases, the patient is ignored and abandoned. If Jesus had been psychotic, most likely he would not have died nailed to a cross as a malefactor, but instead would have been abandoned in the streets.

Why so much hostility?

'The chief priests and the teachers of the law were standing there, vehemently accusing him' (Luke 23:10). A brief chronological perspective will help us to see the evolution of the hostility towards Jesus and the conclusive reason why he was killed. In fact, it started early in his ministry: 'For this reason they tried all the more to kill him; not only was he breaking the Sabbath, but he was even calling God his own Father, making himself equal with God' (John 5:18).

This plot intensified and took shape following the resurrection of Lazarus: 'Here is this man performing many signs. If we let him go on like this, everyone will believe in him . . . So from that day on they plotted to take his life' (John 11:47–48, 53).

Blasphemy is the reason: 'He claimed to be the Son of God'

We arrive at the day of the trial:

> The chief priests and the whole Sanhedrin were looking for false evidence against Jesus so that they could put him to death. But they did not find any, though many false witnesses came forward . . .
>
> But Jesus remained silent.
>
> The high priest said to him . . . 'Tell us if you are the Messiah, the Son of God.'
>
> 'You have said so,' Jesus replied. 'But I say to all of you: from now on you will see the Son of Man sitting at the right hand of the Mighty One and coming on the clouds of heaven.'
> (Matthew 26:59–60, 63–64)

No wonder Caiaphas accused him of blasphemy. In the version recorded by Mark, Jesus affirms literally the divine

'I am' and in both versions quotes the prophecies about the Messiah as being fulfilled in him (Psalm 110:1; Daniel 7:13).

Now they are ready to set the accusation before Pilate: 'The Jewish leaders insisted, "We have a law, and according to that law he must die, because he claimed to be the Son of God"' (John 19:7). It cannot be stated more clearly. The reason for Jesus' confrontation with the religious establishment did not lie in any misconduct due to a psychiatric disorder. What led Jesus to the cross was not insanity on his part, but the hatred of others. The problem wasn't in his head, but rather in the hearts of his enemies. The vehemence with which they accused Jesus and furiously shouted, 'Crucify him, crucify him!' cannot be explained in any other way. No mentally sick person arouses such visceral emotions.

The crown of thorns, the purple robe, the ironical title 'King of the Jews' were intended to mock his pretensions to be the Messiah: 'They . . . twisted together a crown of thorns and set it on his head . . . and mocked him. "Hail, king of the Jews!" they said' (Matthew 27:29). There was no purpose in this whole series of grotesque acts other than to ridicule him in the way that would most humiliate him: his alleged divinity.

Not surprisingly, similar hostility is evident today. 'Mock them, ridicule them,' was the reply Richard Dawkins gave at a gathering when asked how one should respond to a person who believed in God.[6] His words sound like a contemporary echo of the soldiers' mockery. While Jesus cannot be crucified again in a literal way, hatred and offence continue to be weapons against him and his followers. As Ravi Zacharias, the outstanding Christian apologist, commented, 'The hallmark of the so-called "new atheists" is the anger and ridicule that is hurled toward anyone's belief in the sacred.'[7]

Before Pilate: 'Behold the man'
The parody of a trial in the Sanhedrin is now over. There follows another tense, long night: 'Then they spat in his face and struck him with their fists. Others slapped him' (Matthew 26:67). Jesus has to confront the slander of false testimonies, physical violence, torture and humiliation. He does so with courage and composure, meekness and patience, 'in silence, with no word of complaint and no word expressive of pain'.[8] And as if that were not enough, all his own have now abandoned him. Peter denied him that same night and all the disciples fled at the moment of his arrest (Mark 14:50). Jesus is now completely alone, physically lacerated.

At an unusually early hour, around six in the morning, Jesus is brought, bound, before Pilate. The religious leaders seek a speedy authorization for his execution. The trial before the Roman procurator of the province formed the civil part of the case which gave the green light for the execution.

Pilate begins the interrogation of his prisoner: 'Are you the king of the Jews?' (John 18:33). Jesus' response comes in two parts. First, as was his custom, he obliges his interlocutor to think and state his own opinion. So he too asks a question: 'Is that your own idea . . . or did others talk to you about me?' (verse 34).

'My kingdom is not of this world'
Then Jesus introduces an unexpectedly profound twist: 'My kingdom is not of this world. If it were, my servants would fight to prevent my arrest by the Jewish leaders. But now my kingdom is from another place' (verse 36). The interrogation had revolved so far around the political-judicial terrain. Now Jesus gives the dialogue a distinct, much more significant dimension. He moves to the authentic reason not only for the

trial, but also for his life and death. He takes the dialogue from the political to the existential and spiritual. The Master of Galilee declares himself King, not of a human kingdom but rather of a spiritual one.

'The reason I was born and came into the world'

We are now at the climax of the interrogation and one of the culminating points in the life of Jesus. He continues his defence: 'In fact, the reason I was born and came into the world is to testify to the truth. Everyone on the side of truth listens to me' (verse 37).

This is an amazing statement. It is brilliant in its form and wise in its content. In just two phrases, Jesus offers a perfect synthesis of his identity and his work. What mental lucidity! Isn't this the man who had been brutally assaulted and tortured the previous day? Jesus was certainly not immune to the effects of torture, but it is no obstacle for him to demonstrate once more his extraordinary mental sharpness and the coherence of his thinking.

'Ecce homo': 'Behold the man!'

The trial is about to finish. Priests and people clamour for Jesus' blood. Before this, however, Pilate utters a memorable phrase: 'Behold the man!' (KJV), 'Ecce homo'. He was probably not aware of the depth of his sentence, but in these words Pilate sums up who Jesus is: the Man, the true man, the most real and sublime expression of humanity. Even in the midst of his humiliation, bleeding, a crown of thorns girding his head, derided, Jesus remains the human being par excellence. Herod's brutal soldiers had seriously damaged his body, but could not extinguish the radiance of his soul. Indeed, it was through adversity, frustration and suffering that the character of Jesus attained its fullness. What a man!

4. 'The seven words from the cross': Jesus' supreme sermon

During the hours when he was nailed to the cross, Jesus spoke seven times. These memorable utterances, known as 'the seven words', shone like radiant gold in the darkness of those ominous hours. In seven brief sentences a magnificent window opens up to reveal Jesus' extraordinary character and summarize his life. They are the final demonstration of Jesus' mental strength and moral goodness.

Plumbing the depths of these 'seven words' allows us to penetrate the core of Jesus' mind and soul. No wonder the 'seven words' have inspired countless sermons and writings through the centuries. J. S. Bach left us a deeply moving rendition of this biblical text in his *Saint Matthew's Passion*, and Joseph Haydn composed a much-appreciated work, *The Seven Last Words*.

The content of 'the seven words' is impressive in itself, but we are amazed in particular by the order in which they are uttered. This sequence is deeply significant because it is a mirror of Jesus' priorities.

a. A loving heart until the end

Jesus' love and concern for those near him reaches a climax in these utterances. The most natural reaction in the hours leading up to the enactment of a death sentence is introversion. One becomes completely focused on one's own thoughts and emotions, withdrawing from those around. A marked self-centredness is perfectly understandable in such a situation.

But on the cross we see exactly the opposite process: Jesus is oblivious to himself and his own needs (which he will express only at the end), and he focuses his attention on those near him, whether they be his enemies – those who are torturing him – or two unknown malefactors who are being crucified with him, or someone as close to him as his own mother. In each of these three cases, Jesus gives them the precise word they need. In fact, Jesus always speaks to individuals in accordance with their deepest need, just as it was anticipated 800 years before:

> The Sovereign LORD has given me a well-instructed tongue,
>> to know the word that sustains the weary.
> (Isaiah 50:4)

Never has anyone shown such great love at the hour of death. He who claimed to be the Good Shepherd died caring for his sheep. The words of Jesus on the cross are a treasure in which both the essence of his person and the heart of the Christian message are compressed: a deep love towards every single person without discrimination, genuine compassion towards the suffering ones and wisdom to speak words of comfort at the right moment.

In the first three 'words' Jesus shows deep sensitivity to those who are near him (his neighbour) at that moment of great anguish and pain. Let us see how each one received an appropriate word:

b. Words of forgiveness for his enemies

Jesus dies forgiving: 'Father, forgive them, for they do not know what they are doing' (Luke 23:34). This is quite a striking fact. The very last words many people say on their deathbed are: 'Forgive me.' We all have a great need to get rid of our feelings of guilt – especially towards our loved ones – before we, or they, pass away. Remarkably, Jesus had no need to say 'forgive me'. He said exactly the opposite: 'Forgive them.' The reason was not a hardened heart, lacking in awareness of his mistakes, but a clean conscience such that no-one could find any crime in him, as Pilate witnessed repeatedly.

The crucifixion was in itself a supreme act of divine forgiveness towards humankind (John 3:14–15). But it was necessary to make this forgiveness explicit with clear, resonant words, words of overwhelming force and unquestionable spiritual authority. When he cries out, 'Father, forgive them', Jesus articulates the very purpose of his coming into this world. Indeed, his very name 'Jesus' means 'he will save his people from their sins' (Matthew 1:21). His request for forgiveness, therefore, was not only for those who were directly responsible for his unjust death, but for every human being who asked for it, as the impressive song in Isaiah 53 describes vividly.

c. Words of hope for the thief on the cross

Jesus died in the company of two anonymous individuals. These two men had probably never before exchanged words with him. At a certain moment one of them says to Jesus, 'Remember me when you come into your kingdom' (Luke 23:42). Jesus' immediate reply is, once more, a source of comfort: 'Truly I tell you, today you will be with me in Paradise' (23:43). He gives this man what he most needs on the threshold of death: hope. This hope, for sure, was going to be a strong encouragement for him in the endless hours of torture that would follow.

d. Words of protection for his mother

It is highly remarkable that Jesus' last words of care and love for another human being on this earth should have been addressed to his mother: 'When Jesus saw his mother there . . . he said . . . to the disciple [John]: "Here is your mother." And from that time on, this disciple took her into his home' (John 19:26–27). What a meaningful gesture to close a life of service! Jesus had devoted his life entirely to others. Obviously, he could not forget his mother at this time of lacerating pain for her. The heart of Mary was torn apart by the agony of her son. She was desolate in the face of such a tragic end to his life. Furthermore, by that time Mary was probably a widow, and would therefore have been destitute. Jesus did not neglect his duty to 'honour his [father and] mother'.

How human and how divine at the same time! Actually, on the cross we see the two natures of Jesus reaching their maximum expression: truly God and man in one person. In this final act of love, Jesus demonstrates that true spirituality always makes us more human, not less. It is for that reason that Jesus entrusts the care of his mother to his friend and beloved disciple, the sensitive and gentle John, the one who had reclined next to Jesus (John 13:23). John immediately fulfilled this request: 'From that time on, this disciple took her into his home' (John 19:27).

e. His own needs, at the end: 'Later . . . Jesus said . . .'
John now adds a significant remark to the account: 'Later, knowing that everything had now been finished . . .' (John 19:28). So far we have seen how even in his final agony Jesus sought to meet the needs of his neighbour, whether spiritual (salvation and forgiveness) or human and material (the protection of his widowed mother). Only after all this was completed did he give voice to his own needs:

- Physical needs: 'I am thirsty.'
- Emotional and spiritual needs: 'My God, my God, why have you forsaken me?'

Now the agony reaches its highest pitch. A devastating feeling of loneliness lacerates his soul. Jesus feels profoundly lonely because he experiences what it is to be forsaken by God. The awareness that his Father is not nearby becomes an unbearable source of pain for him. Separation from God means an absolute solitude, and this is a hell-like experience. As someone once said, 'Hell is the place where God does not speak any more.'[9]

Jesus' life is about to finish. But before the end, his agony cannot hinder a formidable expression of serenity, trust and hope: 'Father, into your hands I commend my spirit' (Luke 23:46).

Jesus concluded this formidable disclosure of his character with a seventh utterance: 'It is finished.' We cannot think of a better 'epitaph': three ordinary words that summarize an extraordinary life. 'It is finished.' An awesome death sealed an amazing life.

At this point this unique combination of the ordinary – fully human – and the extraordinary – fully divine – makes us feel like the Samaritan woman and paraphrase her words: 'Come, see a man whose death was as unique as his life. Could this be the Messiah?'

8. THE TEST OF INFLUENCE: 'THAT THEY MAY HAVE LIFE, AND HAVE IT TO THE FULL'

I will give you a new heart and put a new spirit in you;
I will remove from you your heart of stone and
give you a heart of flesh.
Ezekiel 36:26

If only we could be a bit more like Jesus,
the world would be transformed.
Bono

We often hear heartfelt phrases, such as 'I wish I could start my life all over again' or 'I so much wish I could be a different person.'

But how could this ever be possible? Transformation is right at the heart of the message of Jesus. Christianity is essentially a matter of changing people, and eventually communities, into the likeness of Jesus. This process has transformed countless millions over the centuries, affecting every part of their lives. This is why Bono's statements on Jesus (both in the epigraph and in the preface) are so relevant to our theme. It is hard to believe that a madman could have had such an astonishing influence on people's lives.

We have reached our last piece of evidence of Jesus' mental health, and it is certainly a key one. It is important because it proves that Jesus' claims are verifiable. One of the strong pieces of evidence in the defence of Jesus' case lies in the verification of his statements and claims. The blind man healed by Jesus responded to those who questioned him with a straightforward reply: 'Whether he is a sinner or not, I don't know. One thing I do know. I was blind but now I see!' (John 9:25). An undeniable change, visible to everyone, was the conclusive proof. The discussion was not about any subjective religious experience, but about the objective evidence of his recovered sight. Likewise, when literally millions of people proclaim that Jesus has entirely transformed their lives and they show evidences of such a change, then we are confronted with a serious argument: Christianity has a verifiable dimension that goes beyond any subjective experience.

Actually, one of the main reasons why Jesus' contemporaries believed in him was precisely because he transformed the lives of people. Through either powerful miracles or quiet personal encounters, men and women were made new. The remarkable fact is that this transforming influence of Jesus continued long after his death. He still powerfully and visibly changes the lives of individuals and, by extension, whole communities.

The purpose of this chapter is to answer the question: how does the Master of Galilee continue to change individuals today? Is it because of his magnetic personality or his radical message of love? Are there any reasons beyond the social or psychological to explain such an unusual influence upon individuals?

His power to change: new life with Jesus

The message of Jesus contains a therapeutic power that brings forth well-being in the deepest sense. This is the reason why it is called the gospel, good news, glad and merry tidings. It runs inseparably with a profound well-being that permeates the whole person and transforms every area of life.

This power operates at three levels: Jesus saves (rescues) us; he changes us; and he heals us. Its effects bring restoration and dignity to the most miserable life. It has no limits because 'the gospel . . . is the power of God that brings salvation to everyone who believes' (Romans 1:16). The word 'power' used here by Paul has the same root as dynamite: a formidable energy that, applied to the human heart, can demolish the highest wall or heal the deepest wound.

A picture is worth a thousand words. In this case, it's not a picture, but real examples of the visible effects of the message of Jesus on individuals and society.

'I do not need these weapons any more': peace instead of violence

In the course of an evangelistic meeting in Chile, the preacher spoke about the power of Jesus to transform hatred and violence into peace and reconciliation. He explained how his forgiveness makes possible this transformation into a new way of life. When the meeting was over, the church steward discovered an abandoned briefcase in the area where the preacher had invited those present to come and pray for this change of life. On opening it, the steward was greatly surprised to find inside a machine gun with ammunition, as well as a bomb. There was also a handwritten note, which read, 'Thank you, now I don't need them. I've understood the message of Jesus to change my life.' The writer of the note happened to be one of the leaders of a terrorist movement in Latin America.

'On the verge of suicide, Jesus stopped me': despair changed into fullness

> I was seriously considering the idea of suicide. I found
> no meaning in life. Nothing satisfied me. If nihilism is
> true, I thought, then we come from nothing and go
> nowhere, and suicide is the only coherent response to life.
> At this stage someone told me about Jesus. As I thoroughly
> examined his life and his message, it appeared to me as the
> only valid alternative to nihilism. It changed my worldview
> dramatically and, subsequently, my life. The despair of
> nihilism was changed into a marvellous comfort and
> quietness.

This is the testimony of an intellectual, now a renowned scholar, and similar experiences are told by many people who, on the verge of suicide, found in Jesus their reason to live.

'My life was a hell': freedom from chains

In the late 1960s and early 1970s a huge number of young people were delivered from the slavery of drugs. A whole generation in the West was trapped in the muddy world of substance abuse, but thousands of them were set free by the power of Jesus. Through the so-called Jesus Movement they came to experience the authenticity of Jesus' claim: 'I will set you free.' In many cases not only the suffering individual was restored, but their families too experienced this transforming power. 'My life was a hell, but Jesus changed it into a confident pilgrimage to heaven,' witnessed a former drug dealer and delinquent.

The same deliverance from all sorts of chains continues today. Men and women enslaved by various kinds of addictions – alcohol, gambling and sexual addiction – find new life in Jesus. Remarkably, the rate of recovery within Christian rehabilitation centres is significantly higher than that at non-Christian ones, to such an extent that in some countries their work is greatly valued – and even supported – by the local authorities.

'Five thousand policemen less': a bottomless well of compassion versus crime and disorder

The work of General William Booth, founder of the Salvation Army,[1] is another example of this transforming 'dynamite'. William and his wife Catherine developed a deep-impact ministry among the marginalized, first in the UK and then in many other parts of the world. They preached the good news of salvation in Jesus among the outcasts, and at the same time offered them 'soup and soap', following the example of Jesus who cared for the whole person. Their son Bramwell believed that his father's greatest power lay in his sympathy, for his heart was 'a bottomless well of compassion'. A Maori woman described William Booth as 'the great grandfather of us all – the man with a thousand hearts in one!' Reflecting Jesus' character was his goal.

No wonder the Booths' work had such a deep influence on society that the famous Baptist preacher Charles Spurgeon once said, 'If the Salvation Army were wiped out of London, five thousand extra policemen could not fill the place in the repression of crime and disorder.'[2]

A striking example of a life more recently rescued from crime is that of Nicky Cruz, leader of the powerful Mau Mau gang in New York. He became a Christian as a result of the work of Teen Challenge.[3] His dramatic life story sounds like a miracle, and is the inspiration behind the book The Cross and the Switchblade, which became the basis for a film of the same name. Here was truly amazing evidence of Jesus' power to make a new person from a shipwrecked life, when nothing else could do so.

'Born again': from the White House to prison, and from prison to Christ

> In one sense I had lost everything – power, prestige, freedom, even my identity. In the summer of 1974, as prisoner 23226 at Maxwell Federal Prison Camp, I stared at the screen of a small black-and-white television set . . . I watched as President Nixon, whom I had faithfully served for three and a half years, resigned his office. It was one of the most desolate experiences of my life. But in another sense I had found everything, all that really matters: a personal relationship with the living God. My life had been dramatically transformed by Jesus Christ.[4]

Charles Colson, known as 'the hatchet man' for Richard Nixon's 'dirty tricks', is another notable example of this new life in Jesus. His journey from a tricky and dissatisfied life to the truth found in Jesus is truly remarkable. He was radically changed when he was 'born again' and began to tell others, even seeking reconciliation with former political enemies. Having been found guilty in the Watergate scandal, he was sentenced and imprisoned. Following his imprisonment and conversion, he founded Prison Fellowship, the largest prison ministry in the USA. He summarized his life thus: 'It is a story of truth, of hope, of the wonderful good news of Jesus Christ's power to change a human life.'[5]

L'Abri communities: shelters for those searching for meaning and identity

Many of the above were wrecked lives from the past that needed a dramatic rescue. But the message of Jesus is not only for those in despair, or the marginalized. Ordinary people from all social conditions, ages, races and cultural backgrounds have come to experience the transforming power of Jesus, because we all have 'a God-shaped void that only God can fill'.[6]

From the 1960s to the 1980s, thousands of young people from all over the world made their way to a small town in Switzerland: 'a pilgrimage perhaps unique in the history of Evangelicalism'.[7] There at L'Abri Fellowship, Francis and Edith Schaeffer provided them with something as unique as it was valuable: an emphasis upon community, and honest answers to life's deepest questions. As a result of the Schaeffers' ministry, many young people found meaning in their life and a new identity in Christ. Quite a number of contemporary Christian leaders were deeply influenced by their encounter with Christ at L'Abri.[8]

In his book *Shining Like Stars*, Lindsay Brown, Christian leader and historian, also tells remarkable stories of Jesus' power to change student lives all over the world, even in some of the toughest social and political arenas. His engaging book depicts graphically how an encounter with Jesus can repair the 'profound sense of dislocation in an age consumed by a quest for identity'.[9]

Likewise, through the work and the prayers of his followers, Jesus transforms communities. One amazing example of this was the Truth and Reconciliation Commission in South Africa. In his description, Archbishop Desmond Tutu, who chaired it, advocated a completely different worldview, that of *ubuntu*, an untranslatable word that implies generosity, sharing, caring: 'It also means my humanity is caught up, is inextricably bound up, in theirs . . . A person is a person through other people . . . I am human because I belong.'[10] Many perpetrators of violence came before the Commission and said, 'I am sorry', and asked for forgiveness from the victims. Apology and remorse were a necessary part of the process. This was an expression of the love of God healing a fractured community, mediated by Archbishop Tutu's Christian leadership.

Individuals and communities long for such transformation because we all greatly need to find answers to the basic questions of life. Jesus responds fully to these questions and thus satisfies the most profound human needs:

- Who am I? Where have I come from? The need for identity.
- What is life? Why am I here? The need for purpose.
- What is there after death? Where do I go? The need for hope.
- What is true? The need for truth.

We will look at identity specifically, and cover the issues of purpose, hope and truth in what follows.

There are indeed many people who are looking for a sense of personal identity within the suffocating crowd that they perpetually feel constrains their actions, speech and even thoughts. Some find their identity in their aloneness away from others, but, as humans, we also feel a need to belong, to be part of our community.

Jesus provides an identity that can survive living in the crowd. 'One in Christ' (Galatians 3:28) expresses our individual identity within the church of Christ; we are 'one with him' (1 Corinthians 6:17), our gift from God as we remain in his care. Together, these provide a unique and an eternal sense of self, controlled not by other people, but by God, and at the same time, we can relate to others. We are in control of our outside circumstances through our faith that God is over all, and we thereby maintain our independence from the crowd.

Christine Ohuruogu's testimony is an excellent illustration of this reality. One of the UK's most successful athletes and a former Olympic and world champion, Christine is also a committed Christian who found her true identity in Christ and the church of Christ:

> For me, faith is a 24/7 thing. It's not something you switch on and off once a week on Sunday. You have to learn to accept yourself and accept who you are in Christ, rather than what other people want you to be . . . Worship services provide me with a place to get spiritual fuel and to re-focus.[11]

How Jesus changes lives

The key question, as we hear about all these changed lives, is: how can it be possible? It is humanly impossible. As the blind man healed by Jesus bluntly put it, 'If this man were not from God, he could do nothing' (John 9:33). There is a supernatural element in this life-changing experience that goes far beyond human efforts or resources. It is not only the message of Jesus per se (his ideas and example) that changes people, but the power of Jesus. We are not dealing merely with the influence of a historical figure – a past event – but with the changing force of a living person. This is why the question of the Samaritan woman with which we finished chapter 7 is critically important: 'Could this be the Messiah?' If Jesus is the Messiah, then we have to refer to him adding a new name: Christ.

This inner transformation is performed not only by the example of Jesus the man, but through the power of Christ, the Son of God. The apostle Paul lucidly articulates this reality in an illuminating statement: 'Therefore, if anyone is in Christ, he is a new creation; the old has passed away, behold, the new has come' (2 Corinthians 5:17, RSV).

Jesus Christ performs a change at three levels:

1. being a new person: I get a *new identity* – Christ lives in me;
2. seeing with different eyes: I get a *new mind* – the mind of Christ moulds me;
3. living a new life: I get *new ethics* – the love of Christ compels me.

This is therefore a holistic transformation: it affects every 'room' of our life, whether existential, emotional or ethical. Christ develops progressively in us a new moral character, which is a mirror of his own character. He also transforms our attitudes, our worldview, because 'the old has passed away'. Now I am able to look at everything and everyone, including myself and my past, with new eyes because 'the new has come'. I live according to a new set of values: new priorities, new objectives, new hopes. Living and loving like Jesus becomes the goal and the privilege of the person who is in Christ. 'Being in Christ' is the only condition (in the next chapter we will see what this means in practice).

The apostle Paul's transformation, which changed him from 'persecutor' (of Christians) to 'persecuted', is a tremendous example of this life-changing power. In his own words,

Whatever were gains to me I now consider loss for the sake of Christ. What is more, I consider everything a loss because of the surpassing worth of knowing Christ Jesus

my Lord, for whose sake I have lost all things. I consider
them garbage, that I may gain Christ.
(Philippians 3:7–8)

Let us focus now in more detail on the outcome of this
change, the consequences in daily life.

A deep well-being described: the power of Jesus' message

Jesus' message, the gospel, brings a unique wholeness, which
is experienced as deep well-being, something we noted at the
start of this chapter. This wholeness is a harmonious and
stable condition that can be portrayed in six wonderful
features. They are not the only ones, but in our opinion these
constitute the backbone of the abundant life Jesus brings:
forgiveness, freedom, purpose, peace, joy and hope. They are
progressive and interdependent, like the steps of a staircase.

Forgiveness

The start of a changed life is forgiveness. This is the first and
necessary step for personal transformation. Jesus cannot
change us if he does not first forgive us from sin: 'For I have
not come to call the righteous, but sinners' (Matthew 9:13).

But what is sin? It is a deep-rooted condition in our heart
that makes us unable to help ourselves by our own efforts.
The original Greek word for 'sin' helps us understand such
inability, with the idea of something that has lost its structure,
a fractured reality that, like a broken bone, is unable to fulfil
its original purpose. In the same way that you cannot walk
with a broken leg, you cannot live a full life if you are fractured
by sin. As a result of this, we live in a permanent 'state
of emergency',[12] a condition that is the opposite of whole-

ness; we feel inwardly broken, split (ambivalent) in our relationships and powerless to live according to the moral standards we wish we could achieve.

Rescue operation for a 'glorious ruin'. Francis Schaeffer describes this condition by saying that 'man is a glorious ruin'. We can still see flashes of this glory, but we are the ruins of a former masterpiece. When the saving power of Jesus transforms this ruin into a new masterpiece, we become 'God's poem',[13] 'created in Christ Jesus to do good works' (Ephesians 2:10).

Therefore, the salvation from sin through Jesus' forgiveness – a rescue operation – becomes the first step, the majestic opening door to a new life. Indeed, once we are forgiven, we get a new perspective in all our relationships: with God, with ourselves and with our neighbour. It is like a window that opens on to a totally different landscape in our life. Reconciliation with God makes possible – and mandatory – the reconciliation with ourselves and with our neighbours. It is here that we start to understand the revolutionary effects of the message of Jesus on individuals and communities. Nothing can be the same again when forgiveness and reconciliation become real.

Transformed people transform their relationships. Our relationships are one of the areas where the changing power of Jesus is shown in its most radical way. Becoming a new person in Christ gives us new relationships, but also new attitudes to our 'old' relationships. As we are transformed, our relationships are also transformed. The statement 'all things are made new' implies that there is no place for resentment, bitterness or hatred any more. Forgiveness and reconciliation are distinct marks of a follower of Jesus. This is why we need to deal with this issue in more detail.

Forgiveness and reconciliation, the source of harmony. There is a close connection between the quality of our relationship with God and the consequent quality of our relationships with other people.[14] Harmony with God is inevitably expressed in harmony with humankind. It is based on forgiveness – being forgiven by God and forgiving other people – and on reconciliation, with God and with others. This has been a distinctive characteristic of Christianity in all its manifestations throughout history. Knowing that one is not forgiven, or not forgiving someone else against whom one holds a grudge, and consequently suffering from a long-term fracture in a close relationship, is a recurring theme among those with mental illness. Jesus spoke directly to all these situations when he taught us to pray, 'Forgive us our debts, as we also have forgiven our debtors' (Matthew 6:12).

Lack of forgiveness has a cost. This, then, is a model for relationships between humans: forgiveness and reconciliation are necessary for harmonious living. But so often this is not achieved. Either the sufferer feels the need to be forgiven by a relative or friend and is never able to obtain forgiveness, or a person is unable to forgive someone else for an event or a series of events that took place long ago, and this continues to prevent any feeling of peace in the present. This gnawing at the heart that occurs with feeling unforgiven or being unable to forgive is at the root of many cases of those suffering from emotional disturbance. To be unforgiven and unable to forgive are different sides of the same coin, and both are extremely destructive of a tranquil and contented mind. Jesus' teaching was to forgive your brother or sister 'not seven times, but seventy-seven times . . . forgive your brother or sister from your heart' (Matthew 18:22, 35).

'Forgiveness gives you freedom': a striking contemporary example. While writing this, the death of Jill Saward was reported in the British national press. At the age of twenty-one she was assaulted and raped at home, in her father's vicarage, by two

intruders, and her father and boyfriend were badly beaten. Following this, she wrote her story and became a prominent campaigner on behalf of victims of rape. She forgave her attackers while fully aware of the enormity of the crime and its effects, and wrote, 'I believe forgiveness gives you freedom. Freedom to move on without being held back by the past.'[15]

Our natural reaction when someone harms us is to retaliate, sometimes disproportionately. If we are not as powerful as the other person, we respond by bearing a grudge, possibly for a very long time. Jesus' forgiveness, 'seventy times seven', is not 'forgive and forget', but passing on the forgiveness we have been given by God to the person who offends us – forgiveness and reconciliation have become our goal.[16] We must forgive others to feel truly forgiven ourselves (Matthew 18:35), and this may be the essential element for the person who is emotionally disturbed.

Forgiving also means healing. Jesus was involved, almost as a therapist, in dealing with Peter's guilt and despair following his triple denial of him. Peter had previously insisted that he would always be loyal to Jesus, even by laying down his life for him (John 13:36–37). But beside the charcoal fire he failed and failed and failed (John 18). His rehabilitation starts by another charcoal fire, by the Sea of Galilee (John 21:9), and Jesus does not forget Peter's sin, but he forgives him – and then gives him a commission, a tremendous sign of trust. This trust is possible through Peter's relationship of love with Jesus. Nowadays this process of forgiving and healing would be described as cognitive behavioural therapy – Peter is able to accept forgiveness and moulds his future behaviour by the command 'feed my sheep', rather than dwelling on past failure; there was no exploration of the past (John 21:15–18). There is a stark contrast between Peter's repentance, following his denials, and subsequent forgiveness and commission, and

Judas's remorse without true repentance or seeking forgiveness, and subsequent suicide, as we saw in chapter 7.

Change is possible. You, the reader, would be fully justified in saying that all this is easier to write about than to put into practice: to achieve change. However, Jesus taught that change is possible, and even the outworking of adverse personality characteristics can be changed. Attitudes and behaviour towards anger, even murder, can be changed by reconciliation, which is a gift of God (Matthew 5:21–26). Forgiveness and reconciliation are fundamental in the relationships between individuals and within the church.

Freedom

A deep feeling of liberation is a hallmark of those transformed lives that we saw earlier. 'Now I am free,' many say with a marked sense of relief. Freedom is the natural consequence of Jesus' forgiveness. The bondage of the fracture (sin) imposed enslavement, but once we are forgiven, we are liberated and able to walk in true freedom.

Referring to himself, Jesus once said to his disciples, 'You will know the truth, and the truth will set you free' (John 8:32). Notice the cause-effect relationship between truth and freedom. There cannot be freedom outside the truth, and Jesus himself claims to be the truth. Freedom is found not in breaking all the alleged ties in your life and doing what you want, but rather in getting to know the truth. Jesus clearly states that the truth is not *something*, but *someone*, a person. This is why he concluded, 'So if the Son [Jesus] sets you free, you will be free indeed' (John 8:36).

Jesus' freedom includes liberation from the burden of a painful past. Our past mistakes and faults do not paralyse us any more. The memories may still be there, but Jesus has removed all poison from these memories. We are also free from the tyranny of others' opinions. Many are dominated by what they think others believe about them: being seen to be 'doing the right thing'. Jesus brings freedom from this bondage by helping us to want to love and serve God, which results in our serving others, but not being controlled by their worldview.

Purpose

Freedom always goes alongside purpose. We are free 'from' in 'order to'. This is also the logical order of Jesus' therapeutic message: he delivers us from sin through forgiveness in order for us to live with a purpose.

As he did with freedom, Jesus associated purpose with himself: 'I am the way and the truth and the life' (John 14:6). Notice how 'the way' and 'the life' – meaning and purpose – revolve again around the truth incarnated in his person. The abundant life Jesus gives – this deep well-being – is the result of being in the truth, because 'There is a thirst which none but he can quench. There is an inner emptiness which none but he can fill.'[17] In other words, Christianity is not true because it works (it changes lives), but it works because it is the truth.

So what is this purpose? Those early disciples, who gave up fishing and walked the hills and valleys of Galilee and travelled to Jerusalem with Jesus, gained a sense of purpose in their lives. It was certainly a missionary purpose – 'go and make disciples' – but it went far beyond a missionary calling. Jesus taught them how to lead their lives – purpose – with the great commandment:

> 'Love the Lord your God with all your heart and with all your soul and with all your mind.' This is the first and greatest commandment. And the second is like it: 'Love

your neighbour as yourself.' All the Law and the Prophets
hang on these two commandments.
(Matthew 22:37–40)

So Jesus made love the DNA of his followers and the core of
their ethics. Experts in sociology and mental health acknowledge that love is the most powerful force for change we have
as humans. The healing and transforming power of love
knows no barriers. This is one of the reasons why the message
of Jesus is so therapeutic: its emphasis on love is unsurpassed.
The Gospel starts with forgiveness, builds upon freedom and
revolves around love.

Therefore, we are dealing not with an *ordinary* self-made
project for life, but with an *extraordinary* God-made purpose
that transcends the here and now, because 'the final place of
life is placed beyond life'.[18]

Peace
By giving us true purpose in life, Jesus brings peace. The
whole bearing of Jesus is peace, and he promises peace to his
followers: 'Peace I leave with you; my peace I give you.'[19] But
he immediately qualified this peace: 'I do not give to you as
the world gives.' In what sense is the peace of Jesus different?
Ordinary peace, 'peace as the world gives', is defined basically
in negative terms: it is the *absence of conflict*, either inner
conflict (anxiety, doubt, shame, guilt) or conflict with others
(broken relationships, quarrels, wars). By contrast, Christ's
peace is something positive: it is a deep harmony inside
oneself that makes it possible to live with difficult and unpleasant outside circumstances. Jesus brings inner peace,
which comes from reconciliation with God – Christians are
no longer under condemnation, having received salvation and
Christ's righteousness.

No wonder the words 'health' and 'peace' come from the same Hebrew root, reminding us of their closeness: real peace is a source of health. It is remarkable in this sense that the World Health Organization's definition of health echoes the biblical concept of peace, *shalom*. It is not only an inner well-being, the subjective dimension, but it also extends to harmony in relationships with others, a personal condition with social implications.

So rich and profound is the peace of Jesus that Paul says that it 'transcends all understanding' (Philippians 4:7).

Joy

Peace and joy go together in the life of Jesus from his birth: 'And the angel said to them, "Be not afraid . . . I bring you good news of a great joy for all the people . . . and on earth peace among men"' (Luke 2:10, 14, RSV). The experience of the shepherds when Jesus was born would eventually be repeated thousands of times in the lives of many others.

Jesus wanted his followers to have the same joy: 'I have told you this so that my joy may be in you and that your joy may be complete' (John 15:11); 'I say these things . . . so that they may have the full measure of my joy within them' (John 17:13). Again, it is not an ordinary joy, but a special one: 'my' joy. Jesus' joy goes beyond fleeting euphoria, a mere gladness. It is a joy inseparably linked to a firm hope. The joy that Jesus gives lies in the conviction that we are not mere survivors in this world, but victors. In the words of Paul, 'in all these things we are more than conquerors through [Christ] who loved us' (Romans 8:37). Joy and hope go together, hand in hand.

Quoting G. K. Chesterton, Ravi Zacharias explains the reason why joy is so natural in a Christian:

For the follower of Jesus, joy is central and sorrow peripheral, while, for the atheist, sorrow is central and joy peripheral. The reason that statement is true is that for the atheist, the foundational questions remain unanswered while they have answers for the peripheral questions . . . For the Christian it is reversed: the foundational questions have been answered and only the peripheral ones remain in doubt . . . Is it any wonder that the Christian faith is the richest faith in music and worship?[20]

Hope

Hope is the gem that crowns this deep well-being. It becomes the antidote to the deepest cause of pessimism and existential despair.

Some of the main thinkers of the past 150 years – Marx, Freud and Nietzsche – share one common feature: the loss of hope. From their teaching we have inherited an age of pessimism and scepticism. Hopelessness permeates the lives of our contemporaries. Actor Marlon Brando reflected this spirit well: 'Life is a mystery and it is an unsolvable one. You just simply live it through and as you draw your last breath you say: "What was that all about?"'[21]

On the other hand, Jesus Christ brings hope into this gloomy panorama. He is indeed the answer to the profound old question: 'Where is the way to the abode of light?' (Job 38:19). Jesus is the way to this light, because he said of himself, 'I am the light of the world' (John 8:12).

Jesus' hope transcends the present. It reaches its climax when he tells his disciples that they will meet again after death: 'You will grieve, but your grief will turn to joy . . . now is your time of grief, but I will see you again and you will rejoice, and no one will take away your joy' (John 16:20–22). In Jesus' hope the best part is yet to come: a glorious future –

a new heaven and a new earth – lies ahead. Victory over death and his promise of eternal life were based not on utopia, but on the historical facts that would follow during and after his own death. No wonder that the very first words to announce the birth of Jesus were: 'Comfort, comfort my people' (Isaiah 40:1).

This well-being can be summarized thus: abundant life or life to the full. 'I came that they may have life, and have it abundantly,' Jesus stated (John 10:10, RSV). The word 'abundant' in the original may also mean 'superior', 'a better quality'. Jesus' new life is superior, or 'to the full', because it enables us to rebuild the very foundations of our existence by giving us back the true purpose of life: relationship with our Creator. It is superior also because it meets our deepest needs – identity and meaning – thereby providing authentic self-fulfilment.

The apostle Peter, quoting Psalm 16:11, in his sermon at Pentecost, makes a formidable summary of the uniqueness of Jesus' well-being:

> You have made known to me the paths of life;
>   you will fill me with joy in your presence.
> (Acts 2:28)

What a precise description of the change Jesus operates! Finding the path of life and being filled with joy are two of the most basic longings of human beings. They are met only in Jesus' presence.

For all these reasons, we are persuaded that the message of Jesus contains a unique therapeutic element for which there is no substitute. As psychiatrists, we are eyewitnesses of this healing power. 'There is a deep *hidden room* in our hearts that no psychiatric expertise, or human resource, can reach. It is a room related to our meaning in life and to our thirst for eternity.'[22]

One of us (Andrew) was an atheist at the age of eighteen. Over a few months I was drawn to faith in Jesus Christ, and soon after, as a medical student, believed that I should enter psychiatry. As a psychiatrist, I have always considered that my faith should influence and contribute to my psychiatric practice. And both of us identify with the Spanish pastor and thinker who described his own experience with Jesus with these powerful words: 'I was captivated and captured by Christ.'[23] This was his response – and ours – to the attractiveness of the person and message of the Master of Galilee.

Jesus said, 'Follow me' to very different kinds of people and he changed the course of their lives. He makes the same call today, 2,000 years later. Answering this call is the way to discover, and fully live out, the central purpose of our existence. As St Augustine said, 'You have made us for yourself, O Lord, and our hearts are restless until they find their rest in you.'[24] This is the reason why our lives can only be rebuilt by the one who promised, 'I will give you a new heart and put a new spirit in you' (Ezekiel 36:26).

Now, after considering what Jesus intends – and is able – to make of us, a vital question needs to be answered. It is the question that Pilate asked before handing him over to be crucified: 'What shall I do, then, with Jesus?' (Matthew 27:22). Answering this question requires a knowledge of the claims Jesus made for himself. To this crucial issue we will now turn.

9. THE TEST OF HIS CLAIMS: 'WHO DO YOU SAY I AM?'

> *The discrepancy between the depth and sanity . . . of*
> *Jesus' moral teaching and the rampant megalomania*
> *which must lie behind His theological teaching has never*
> *been satisfactorily got over unless He is indeed God.*
> C. S. Lewis

'Who do you claim to be?' (John 8:53, RSV). With this compelling question the Jewish religious leaders, full of rage, challenged Jesus to define once and for all who he really was. They had just accused him of being demon possessed as well as an impostor. There was something in Jesus' teaching that was too annoying to their ears, and too threatening to their interests. It was time to make a decision and act accordingly.

We have dealt so far with some key questions that highlight the person of Jesus: what was his character like? How did he live? How did he relate to others? How did he react to adversity? How could he change people's lives? But a fundamental question is missing: what did Jesus really think of himself?

The problem of Jesus' claims leads us to the great paradox that we anticipated in the preface. Solving this paradox gave us, the authors, the clue to a fuller understanding of the uniqueness of Jesus' life and work. Nevertheless, as we said in the beginning, this issue goes beyond an intellectual question to become a personal challenge. It poses before us a dilemma that requires both an answer and a commitment. We now come to the most decisive moment on the journey.

The great paradox

In a sense, the Jews were right in their puzzlement. Something in Jesus is disturbing. He was constantly talking about himself; his teaching often revolved around his own person. Actually, he openly accepted this fact. When they accuse him, 'Here you are, appearing as your own witness' (literally, 'you witness about yourself'), Jesus does not deny it, but he plainly confirms their accusation: 'I am the one who testifies for myself . . .' (John 8:13, 18). As Carnegie Simpson puts it, 'Alone, absolutely alone, among leaders of the soul, Jesus absorbs the highest principles into his own personality.'[1]

There is, therefore, a striking discrepancy between the humility of the servant and the greatness of the Lord, his self-abasement and his high sense of self. While the 'you' was the centre of his ministry, the 'me' – 'I am' – was the axis of his message. In terms of service, others always came first and he was last, but in terms of self-concept, he placed himself in the forefront. This is the paradox that baffles us: the contrast between the seeming self-centredness of his teachings and the self-denial of his conduct. Let us focus on one outstanding example.

'Lord, are you going to wash my feet?' Peter's astonishment was very understandable. The Master was behaving like a slave. This remarkable event (John 13:1–17) accurately exemplifies the paradox of Jesus. Shortly before his death the teacher and Lord girded himself with a towel, knelt and washed the feet of his disciples. As John Stott says,

> Is this not unique in the history of the world? There have been lots of arrogant people, but they all behaved like it. There have also been humble people, but they have not made great claims for themselves. It is the combination of egocentricity and humility that is so startling . . . Why am I a Christian? Intellectually speaking . . . it is because he who claimed to be his disciples' Lord humbled himself to be their servant.[2]

We are faced with a great paradox that needs an explanation. C. S. Lewis hints at the answer when he says, 'The discrepancy . . . has never been satisfactorily got over unless He is indeed God.'[3]

A brief review of Jesus' claims will help us understand this paradox and, at the same time, will fully disclose his identity and its implications. We turn, therefore, to the opening question: 'Who do you claim to be?' Let Jesus himself give the answer.

The great claims

Jesus said, 'I am the way and the truth and the life. No one comes to the Father except through me' (John 14:6). The claims of Jesus regarding his identity are clearly defined in seven striking statements that begin with the words 'I am'. On different occasions in the Gospel of John Jesus explains who he is, using simple but powerful metaphors:

1. 'I am the bread of life.'
2. 'I am the light of the world.'
3. 'I am the gate of the sheep.'

4. 'I am the good shepherd.'
5. 'I am the resurrection and the life.'
6. 'I am the way and the truth and the life.'
7. 'I am the true vine.'

From these statements we draw four decisive conclusions that are related, with one leading to the other.

He claims to be God: 'I and the Father are one' (John 10:30)

First of all, Jesus makes himself equal to God. Remember that the religious leaders decided to kill him as soon as they found out that 'he was even calling God his own Father, making himself equal with God' (John 5:18). Actually, the very words 'I am', which head each one of these utterances, clearly point to his divine nature. 'I am' was the name reserved exclusively for God. When the Jews confronted him with the question, 'Who do you think you are?', Jesus replied, 'Before Abraham was born, I am!' (John 8:58). This response alludes unequivocally to both his deity and his eternity. No wonder that the reaction this provoked from the Jews was an attempt to lynch him (John 8:59).

This first claim becomes the basis for the other three.

He claims to give abundant and eternal life

On the basis that he is God, Jesus also claims that he is able to give life, and to guide us to eternal life: 'I am the living bread that came down from heaven. Whoever eats this bread will live for ever' (John 6:51). He openly asserts that he can meet the most profound human needs. Notice these unusual statements:

- 'I am the bread of life. Whoever comes to me will never go hungry, and whoever believes in me will never be thirsty' (John 6:35, 58).

- 'On the last and greatest day of the festival, Jesus stood and said in a loud voice, "Let anyone who is thirsty come to me and drink. Whoever believes in me . . . rivers of living water will flow from within them"' (John 7:37–38).
- 'Very truly I tell you, whoever obeys my word will never see death' (John 8:51).

Remarkably, each of the seven 'I am' utterances contains a life-giving message. The bread, the light, the shelter of the gate, the guidance of the shepherd, the hope beyond death – all these illustrations point to fullness of life here and now, but also for all eternity (as seen in the last chapter).

He claims to be Saviour and Lord

How does Jesus intend to give life? His first two claims were not for the purpose of inflating his ego, like some paranoid or narcissistic individual, but rather of saving like a servant. The reason for his life was to demolish all walls of separation, and thus reconcile humankind with God, and with one another: 'For the Son of Man came to seek and to save the lost' (Luke 19:10). This could only be accomplished by the most striking paradox: his humiliating death as a servant in order to be exalted to the highest as Lord: 'You call me "Teacher" and "Lord," and rightly so, for that is what I am' (John 13:13; see also Philippians 2:9–11).

A notable feature of these claims is that Jesus never intended them to be for his own benefit or glory: 'I am not seeking glory for myself . . . If I glorify myself, my glory means nothing' (John 8:50, 54). There is no personal gain whatsoever in promises such as 'I will set you free', 'I will give you rest', 'I will give you peace' or 'I am going to my Father's house to prepare a place for you.' His claims may seem arrogant, but they were always meant to bless and benefit others, their target being the 'you', not the 'ego'. They sound self-centred, but they are not selfish.

Amazing claims! Through all these brilliant metaphors we clearly perceive the depth and sanity of Jesus' mind and heart. A strong willingness to serve and to save: this is the core of his identity. Such lucid thought and such a warm heart remain very distant from the deluded confusion of psychosis, the self-glorification of paranoia or the self-interest of an impostor!

But can we trust his words? What is it that makes his claims reliable? Jesus himself gives the answer, the guarantee that his claims and promises are utterly trustworthy.

He claims to have risen from the dead

The proof that legitimizes these claims is the resurrection of Jesus: 'I am the resurrection and the life. The one who believes in me will live, even though they die' (John 11:25).

Here is not the place to consider whether it happened as described in the Gospel narratives – many have done this and written convincingly on the subject.[4] Suffice it to say here, 'The resurrection is not a belief that arose within the Church; it is rather the belief around which the Church itself was born and grew.'[5]

The key question for us is: does it really matter? Does it make any difference to us if the crucifixion was followed by the resurrection? According to the apostle Paul, it matters indeed, because 'if Christ has not been raised . . . we are of all people most to be pitied' (1 Corinthians 15:14, 19). It matters also because Jesus himself claims that because of his resurrection he will eventually raise from the dead all those who believe in him: 'Whoever eats my flesh and drinks my blood has eternal life, and I will raise them up at the last day'

(John 6:54). Actually, Jesus is so emphatic about this idea that he repeats it four times in the same discourse (John 6:39, 40, 44, 54).

The great challenge: 'Who do *you* say I am?'

If Jesus was not mentally disturbed and he was not an impostor either, if we agree that 'he comes before us . . . as the most balanced and integrated of human beings',[6] then, as pointed in our initial dilemma, only one option remains: his claims are true, and he was indeed what he declared himself to be: God.

This conclusion, however, presents us with a radical challenge: his demands clearly require not only intellectual acceptance, but personal commitment. For this reason we ultimately have to answer the same question with which Jesus confronted his disciples: 'Who do you say I am?'

We now come to a point when it is not we ourselves who 'evaluate' Jesus any more, but Jesus himself is the one who interrogates us with his compelling question.

Why is it a compelling question? To answer the inquiry, 'Who do you say I am?', is not just a matter of 'having an opinion about', but a matter of 'follow me', as he often urged his disciples to do. You cannot respond to it only with your head, but with your heart. Jesus' claims go beyond *intellectual* knowledge; they demand *experiential* knowledge, the kind of knowledge that comes only from a personal encounter, a first-hand experience. It is not enough to be 'amazed at Jesus', as many of his contemporaries were, because Jesus wants not to be admired, but to be loved. Personal allegiance is the ultimate consequence of Jesus' claims.

Therefore, getting to know Jesus means not only being informed about him, but being transformed by him. This is why he wants this personal encounter to be the first step of a lifelong walk, the starting point of a personal relationship. So here again is a journey that is not one, as earlier, of exploration and detective work; rather, it engages our deepest selves.

Once more, Jesus is very radical when he claims, 'I am the vine; you are the branches. If you remain in me and I in you, you will bear much fruit; apart from me you can do nothing' (John 15:5). Jesus never intended to establish a new religion, but to start a new relationship with anyone who wishes to embark on it.

We can bear witness to this life-transforming experience. As psychiatrists, our professional judgment allows us to affirm that we do not see in Jesus the slightest shadow of mental imbalance. But our conclusion about the Master of Galilee goes far beyond this professional assertion. As we said in the preface, we have discovered over the years not only Jesus' unique emotional stability and his enormous moral stature, but also his power to give life and give it to the full. We have found in Jesus the deepest meaning for our existence here and now, and a firm hope for the life to come. For all these reasons he has attracted us in such a way that we have experienced what he claimed of himself: 'And, when I am lifted up from the earth, I will draw [attract] all people to myself' (John 12:32).

We therefore identify with the words of Malcolm Muggeridge:

It is precisely when every earthly hope has been explored and found wanting, when every possibility of help from earthly sources has been sought and is not forthcoming, when every recourse this world offers, moral as well as material, has been explored to no effect . . . and in the gathering darkness every glimmer of light has finally flickered out – it is then that

Christ's words bring their inexpressible comfort, that his light shines brightest, abolishing the darkness forever.[7]

It is the light of the one who said, 'Here I am! I stand at the door and knock. If anyone hears my voice and opens the door, I will come in and eat with that person, and they with me' (Revelation 3:20).[8]

A prayer

Lord Jesus Christ,
I am convinced that you are, and were, the healthiest mind of all, and wholly trustworthy in every aspect of life. I believe that your claims are true, that you are God, that you died for my sins, and that you have risen and triumphed over death. Thank you for giving life to the full, your loving offer of forgiveness, freedom and purpose,

I am aware that before I even started looking for you, you were already seeking me and drawing me to you. Now I have heard you knocking at my door and I ask you to come into my life as my Saviour and my Lord, and remain with me. I want to follow you every day of my life.

Amen

NOTES

Foreword

1. Sigmund Freud (1856–1939), *The Future of an Illusion* (1927).
2. Andrew Sims, *Is Faith Delusion? Why Religion Is Good for Your Health* (Continuum, 2009), p. 221.
3. Ibid., p. 100.
4. C. S. Lewis, *Mere Christianity* (William Collins, 1952), pp. 55–56.

Preface

1. Fyodor Dostoevsky, in 'Letter To Mme. N. D. Fonvisin' (1854), as published in *Letters of Fyodor Michailovitch Dostoyevsky to His Family and Friends* (1914), Letter XXI.
2. The idea of the trilemma, however, must be attributed to G. K. Chesterton (*The Everlasting Man*). C. S. Lewis, who was a great admirer of Chesterton, popularized it. For this reason, while acknowledging Chesterton's original

authorship, we will refer from now onwards to 'the
C. S. Lewis trilemma'.

Introduction

1. The purpose and nature of this book do not allow us to
   consider issues like the reliability of the New Testament
   documents or the debate over the historical Jesus. For a further
   study of these subjects, see the suggested reading at the end
   of the book.
2. Oliver Barclay, *Reasons for Faith* (IVP, 1974), p. 80.
3. P. Carnegie Simpson, *The Fact of Christ* (Hodder & Stoughton,
   1935), pp. 34–35.
4. We, the authors, subscribe to the 'Chalcedonian Definition' of
   AD 451, the standard, orthodox definition of the biblical teaching
   on the person of Christ. See the whole statement in Wayne
   Grudem, *Systematic Theology* (Zondervan, 1994), p. 556. For
   further reading on Christology, see also the recommended
   bibliography at the end of the book.

1. The test of psychiatry

1. Mark 8:29, 31; 9:9; 14:62; 15:15.
2. Tom Wright, *Simply Jesus: Who He Was, What He Did, Why
   It Matters* (SPCK, 2011), p. 165.
3. John Stott, *Through the Bible, Through the Year: Daily Reflections
   from Genesis to Revelation* (Candle Books, 2006), pp. 133–140.
4. Tom Wright, *John for Everyone: Part 2* (SPCK, 2002), p. 41.
5. Ibid., pp. 61–62.
6. Andrew Sims, *Symptoms in the Mind: An Introduction to Descriptive
   Psychopathology*, 3rd edn (Saunders, 2003), p. 411.
7. Tom Wright, *John for Everyone: Part 1* (SPCK, 2002), p. 42.
8. Wright, *John for Everyone: Part 2* (SPCK, 2002), p. 88.

2. The test of psychosis

1. R. Alan Cole, *Mark: An Introduction and Commentary*, Tyndale New Testament Commentaries (Tyndale Press, 1961), pp. 82–83.

2. P. F. Liddle, 'Descriptive clinical features of schizophrenia', in M. G. Gelder, N. C. Andreasen, J. J. López-Ibor, Jr and J. R. Geddes (eds.), *New Oxford Textbook of Psychiatry*, 2nd edn (Oxford University Press, 2009), p. 528.

3. P. Bech, 'Clinical features of mood disorders and mania', in M. G. Gelder, N. C. Andreasen, J. J. López-Ibor Jr and J. R. Geddes (eds.), *New Oxford Textbook of Psychiatry*, 2nd edn (Oxford University Press, 2009), p. 636.

4. A. Munro, 'Persistent delusional symptoms and disorders', in *New Oxford Textbook of Psychiatry*, p. 612.

5. Andrew Sims, *Symptoms in the Mind: An Introduction to Descriptive Psychopathology*, 3rd edn (Saunders, 2003), p. 149.

6. Ibid., p. 117.

7. J. E. D. Esquirol (1817), *Hallucinations*, reprinted in *Des Maladies Mentales* (Baillière, 1938).

8. Tom Wright, *Luke for Everyone* (SPCK, 2001), p. 43.

9. Matthew 17:1–9; Mark 9:2–8; Luke 9:28–36.

10. Sims, *Symptoms in the Mind*, pp. 155–156.

11. The Archbishop's Council, *The Order for the Celebration of Holy Communion, Order One* (Church House Publishing, 2000), p. 15.

12. Andrew Sims, *Is Faith Delusion?* (Continuum, 2009), pp. 132–133.

13. Ibid., pp. 37, 38.

3. The test of mental impairment

1. Affirming the full humanity of Jesus has always been an important issue for historic Christianity. From the beginning some said that Jesus was not really a man, but only seemed to

be one. This heresy, called Docetism (from the Greek *dokein*, 'to seem, to appear to be'), was addressed by the apostle John in his first epistle (1 John 4:2–3).

2. Tom Wright, *John for Everyone: Part 2* (SPCK, 2002), pp. 10–11.

3. John 13:23; 19:26; 20:2; 21:7, 20.

4. C. M. Parkes, 'The psychological reaction to loss of a limb: The first year after amputation', in J. G. Howells (ed.), *Modern Perception in the Psychiatric Aspects of Surgery* (Macmillan, 1976), pp. 515–533.

5. G. L. Engel, 'A life setting conducive to illness: The giving up–given up complex', *Annals of International Medicine* 69 (1968), pp. 293–300.

6. D. M. Clark, 'Cognitive behaviour therapy for anxiety disorders', in M. G. Gelder, N. C. Andreasen, J. J. López-Ibor, Jr and J. R. Geddes (eds.), *New Oxford Textbook of Psychiatry*, 2nd edn (Oxford University Press, 2009), pp. 1285–1298.

7. Christopher Williams, Paul Richards and Ingrid Whitton, *I'm Not Supposed to Feel Like This* (Hodder & Stoughton, 2002).

8. D. G. Myers and E. Denier, 'The pursuit of happiness: New research uncovers some non-intuitive insights into how many people are happy – and why', *Scientific American* 274 (1996), pp. 54–56.

9. Tom Whipple, 'American psycho on path to power', *The Times*, 23 August 2016, <www.thetimes.co.uk/article/american-psycho-on-path-to-power-w5nw2fnmh> (accessed 11 Decmber 2017).

10. Kurt Schneider, *Psychopathic Personalities*, 9th edn trans. M. W. Hamilton, 1958 (Cassell, 1950).

11. See the work of Jack Dominian, one of our few predecessors as a Christian writer and psychiatrist, e.g. *One Like Us: A Psychological Interpretation of Jesus* (Darton, Longman & Todd, 1998).

12. Schneider, *Psychopathic Personalities*.

13. World Health Organization, *The ICD 10 Classification of Mental and Behavioral Disorders: Clinical Descriptions and Guidelines* (World Health Organization, 1992).

14. American Psychiatric Association, *Diagnostic and Statistical Manual of Mental Disorders*, 5th edn (American Psychiatric Association, 2013).

15. Ibid.

16. F. R. Volkmar and A. Klin, 'Autism and the pervasive developmental disorders', in M. G. Gelder, N. C. Andreasen, J. J. López-Ibor, Jr and J. R. Geddes (eds.), *New Oxford Textbook of Psychiatry*, 2nd edn (Oxford University Press, 2009), p. 528.

4. The test of his character

1. 'What Life Means to Einstein: An Interview by George Sylvester Viereck', *The Saturday Evening Post*, 26 October 1929, p. 17.

2. 'Letter To Mme. N. D. Fonvisin' (1854), as published in *Letters of Fyodor Michailovitch Dostoyevsky to His Family and Friends* (1914), Letter XXI.

3. John Stott, *The Message of Ephesians*, The Bible Speaks Today (Inter-Varsity Press, 1979), p. 148.

4. Friedrich Nietzsche, in *The Anti-Christ* (1895), thrusts Christian morality upside down, claiming that the only true moral good is 'the will to power', and weakness the only true evil.

5. For a further study of Jesus as a servant, see Isaiah 42 – 53, a section known as 'The songs of the servant', four poems that prophetically describe the character and work of Jesus 800 years in advance.

6. It is a pathology that falls into the category of impulse-control disorders. The condition is characterized by a failure to resist aggressive impulses, resulting in harm to others.

7. Armand M. Nicholi, Jr, *The Harvard Guide to Modern Psychiatry* (Harvard University Press, 1978), p. 2.

8. Ibid., p. 3.

9. *The Hiding Place* (Hodder & Stoughton, 1972) is the title given to the account of Corrie ten Boom's war experiences.

10. L. Wilson, 'Corrie ten Boom', in Timothy Larsen (ed.), *Biographical Dictionary of Evangelicals* (Inter-Varsity Press, 2003), p. 664.

11. Nova is the name given to a star that suddenly becomes thousands of times brighter. The author is referring to the extraordinary power of grace.

12. Philip Yancey, *What's So Amazing about Grace?* (Zondervan, 1997), p. 30.

13. Joseph Ratzinger, *La infancia de Jesús* (Planeta, 2012), p. 129.

14. John Stott, *Through the Bible, Through the Year: Daily Reflections from Genesis to Revelation* (Candle Books, 2006), p. 177.

15. Os Guinness, *Impossible People: Christian Courage and the Struggle for the Soul of Civilization* (InterVarsity Press, 2016), p. 32.

16. Millard J. Erickson, *Christian Theology* (Baker Academic, 1985), p. 736. This idea reminds us that the human nature of Jesus was exactly like our human nature, yet without sin, as stated in the Creed of Chalcedon: 'Consubstantial with us according to the Manhood; in all things like unto us, without sin'.

5. The test of a consistent life

1. Quotation attributed to Abraham Lincoln among others, but the French minister and writer Jacques Abbadie should probably be credited with the original statement.

2. John Stott, *Through the Bible, Through the Year: Daily Reflections from Genesis to Revelation* (Candle Books, 2006), p. 179.

3. Joseph Ratzinger, *La infancia de Jesús* (Planeta, 2012), p. 126.

4. For a deeper study of this subject, read John Stott, *'But I Say to You . . .': Christ the Controversialist* (Inter-Varsity Press, 2013).

5. Malcolm Muggeridge, *Jesus Rediscovered* (Fontana, 1969), p. 78.

6. James T. Fisher, *A Few Buttons Missing: The Case Book of a Psychiatrist* (J. B. Lippincott, 1951), p. 273.

7. The salt and light metaphors indicate the influence for good that a Christian is called to exert in the world. The salt prevents decay; the light illuminates in darkness.

8. John Stott, 'Evangelism and Social Responsibility', *Southern Cross*, October 1980, p. 23.

9. For a fresh glimpse of this facet of Jesus' character, see David Stevens and Gregg Lewis, *Jesus, M.D.: A Doctor Examines the Great Physician* (Zondervan, 2001).

10. The motto of the ancient physicians was *Vir bonus, peritus curandi*: a good person, expert in healing.

11. 'Medicine of the person', founded by Paul Tournier, a Swiss physician and author, is an approach to medical practice dedicated to treating patients with an awareness of the whole person.

6. The test of relationships

1. This is why the social dimension is emphasized in the current concept of health, the so-called biopsychosocial model. Health is measured also in terms of relationships.

2. John Stott is considered one of the most outstanding Christian leaders of the twentieth century. A world-renowned author, pastor and theologian, he was named by *Time* magazine in 2005 as one of the 100 most influential people in the world.

3. Alfred Edersheim, *The Life and Times of Jesus the Messiah* (Hendrickson, 1992), p. 414.

4. David Cranston, *On Eagle's Wings: Models in Mentoring* (Regnum Books International, 2014), p. 20.

5. For a deeper study of the richness of John 13 – 17, we recommend David Gooding, *In the School of Christ* (Myrtlefield House, 1998).

7. The test of adversity

1. Paul E. Little, *Know Why You Believe* (InterVarsity Press, 2008), p. 53.
2. Joni Eareckson Tada, *Diamonds in the Dust: 366 Sparkling Devotions* (Zondervan, 1993), in entry for 11 February.
3. G. Campbell Morgan, *The Great Physician: The Method of Jesus with Individuals* (Marshall, Morgan & Scott, 1953), p. 42.
4. Alfred Edersheim, *The Life and Times of Jesus the Messiah*, vol. II, (Hendrickson, 1992), p. 538.
5. The medical explanation of this phenomenon is that blood flows out of the small blood vessels, the capillaries, when there is a very intense state of stress.
6. Quoted in Ravi Zacharias and Vince Vitale, *Jesus among Secular Gods: The Countercultural Claims of Christ* (FaithWords, 2017), p. 2.
7. Ibid., p. 3.
8. G. Campbell Morgan, *The Crises of the Christ* (Pickering & Inglis, 1954), p. 214.
9. Attributed to Dostoyevsky.

8. The test of influence

1. The Salvation Army is considered to be one of the largest Protestant charities in the world.
2. Henry Gariepy, *Christianity in Action: The International History of the Salvation Army* (Eerdmans, 2009), p. 57.
3. Teen Challenge, founded by David Wilkerson, is an agency dedicated to the rehabilitation of inner-city young people, especially teenagers with chemical dependencies and debilitating lifestyles.
4. From Colson's autobiography, Charles W. Colson, *Born Again* (Baker, 2008), p. 6.

5. Ibid., p. 7.

6. Attributed to Blaise Pascal, *Pensées*, VII (425), published 1670.

7. Timothy Larsen (ed.), *Biographical Dictionary of Evangelicals* (Inter-Varsity Press, 2003), p. 583.

8. L'Abri today perpetuates the vision of Francis Schaeffer in several countries to provide 'a shelter' and the opportunity to seek answers to honest questions about God and the significance of human life.

9. Lindsay Brown, *Shining Like Stars: The Power of the Gospel in the World's Universities* (Inter-Varsity Press, 2006), p. 10.

10. Desmond Tutu, *No Future without Forgiveness* (Rider, 1999), pp. 34–35.

11. Interview with Christine at Keep the Faith, <www.keepthefaith. co.uk/2013/09/29/interview-with-christine-ohuruogu-2> (accessed 12 December 2017).

12. An expression used by Harry Blamires, in *Recovering the Christian Mind: Meeting the Challenge of Secularism* (InterVarsity Press, 1988), p. 14.

13. In the original Greek, the word *poiema*, translated 'workmanship' (NIV), literally means 'poem'.

14. Andrew Sims, *Is Faith Delusion?* (Continuum, 2009), pp. 38–42.

15. You can read Jill's story at <www.bbc.co.uk/stoke/ insidelives/2004/06/jill_saward.shtml> (accessed 12 December 2017).

16. Tom Wright, *Matthew for Everyone: Part 2* (SPCK, 2002), p. 39.

17. Roger Steer, *Inside Story: The Life of John Stott* (Inter-Varsity Press, 2009), p. 263.

18. Alexis de Tocqueville, quoted by Os Guiness, *The Call: Finding and Fulfilling the Central Purpose of Your Life* (Spring Harvest/ Paternoster, 2001), p. 6.

19. John 14:27; 16:33; 20:19, 21.

20. Ravi Zacharias and Vince Vitale, *Jesus among Secular Gods: The Countercultural Claims of Christ* (FaithWords, 2017), pp. 6–7, 60.

21. Quoted by Robert Crawford, *Can We Ever Kill? An Ethical Enquiry* (Fount, 1991), p. 149.
22. Pablo Martinez, in David J. Randall (ed.), *Why I Am Not an Atheist: Facing the Inadequacies of Unbelief* (Christian Focus, 2013), p. 111.
23. The words of the Revd José M. Martinez, father of Pablo Martinez.
24. *St Augustine, Confessions, Book 1.*

9. The test of his claims

1. P. Carnegie Simpson, *The Fact of Christ* (Hodder & Stoughton, 1935), p. 11.
2. John Stott, *Why I Am a Christian* (Inter-Varsity Press, Leicester, 2003), p. 46.
3. C. S. Lewis, *Miracles* (Macmillan, 1960), pp. 108–109.
4. For a further study of this subject, we recommend *Who Moved the Stone?* by Frank Morison (Zondervan, 1987). This 1930s classic has been reprinted many times. The author set out to disprove the resurrection of Jesus, by analysing the Scriptures and historical documents, but he became a firm believer. Another excellent contribution was made more recently by Professor John Lennox in *Gunning for God: Why New Atheists Are Missing the Target* (Lion, 2011). The chapter 'Did Jesus rise from the dead?' (and indeed the whole book) is a robust biblical response to the arguments of New Atheism.
5. C. H. Dodd, quoted by Philip Yancey, *El Jesús que nunca conocí (The Jesus I never knew)* (Editorial Vida, 1996), p. 220.
6. Stott, *Why I Am a Christian*, p. 45.
7. Malcolm Muggeridge, quoted in Roger Steer, *Inside Story: The Life of John Stott* (Inter-Varsity Press, 2009), p. 181.
8. These penetrating words, originally addressed to the believers of the church in Laodicea, have touched the hearts of thousands who have opened the door of their lives to Jesus, inviting him to come in as their Saviour and Lord.

FURTHER READING AND RESOURCES

Recommended reading

F. F. Bruce, *The New Testament Documents: Are They Reliable?* (Eerdmans, 2003)

Richard Cunningham, *Resurrection: Fact or Fiction?* (UCCF: The Christian Unions, 2015)

Sharon Dirckx, *Why? Looking at God, Evil and Personal Suffering* (Inter-Varsity Press, 2013)

Os Guinness, *Impossible People: Christian Courage and the Struggle for the Soul of Civilization* (InterVarsity Press, 2016)

William Lane Craig, *Reasonable Faith: Christian Truth and Apologetics*, 3rd edn (Crossway, 2008)

John Lennox, *Gunning for God: Why the New Atheists Are Missing the Target* (Lion Books, 2011)

C. S. Lewis, *Mere Christianity* (William Collins, 1952)

Frank Morison, *Who Moved the Stone?* (Zondervan, 1987)

Amy Orr-Ewing, *Why Trust the Bible? Answers to 10 Tough Questions* (Inter-Varsity Press, 2008)

Michael Ots, *What Kind of God? Responding to 10 Popular Accusations* (Inter-Varsity Press, 2011)

Rebecca Manley Pippert, *Hope Has Its Reasons: The Search to Satisfy Our Deepest Longings* (InterVarsity Press, 2010)

Rebecca Manley Pippert, *Discovering the Real Jesus* (The Good Book Company, 2016)

John Stott, *Basic Christianity* (Inter-Varsity Press, 1958)

John Stott, *Why I Am a Christian* (Inter-Varsity Press, 2003)

Lee Strobel, *The Case for Christ: A Journalist's Personal Investigation of the Evidence for Jesus* (Zondervan, 1998)

Ravi Zacharias and Vince Vitale, *Jesus among Secular Gods: The Countercultural Claims of Christ* (Faith Words, 2017)

Resources from the authors

Dr Pablo Martinez

More information about the work of Dr Pablo Martinez may be found at Christian Thought, <www.christian-thought.org>. His books, articles, recorded lectures and other resources are available on this website, founded by his father, the Revd José M. Martinez, a respected theologian and Christian leader in the Spanish-speaking world.

Professor Andrew Sims

Is Faith Delusion? Why Religion Is Good for Your Health (Continuum, 2009)

Symptoms in the Mind: An Introduction to Descriptive Psychopathology (Saunders, 1988)

Printed and bound by CPI Group (UK) Ltd, Croydon, CR0 4YY

13/04/2025

14656475-0004